THE SURPRISING
SCIENCE OF MEETINGS

THE SURPRISING SCIENCE OF MEETINGS

HOW YOU CAN LEAD YOUR
TEAM TO PEAK PERFORMANCE

STEVEN G. ROGELBERG

OXFORD
UNIVERSITY PRESS

OXFORD
UNIVERSITY PRESS

Oxford University Press is a department of the University of Oxford. It furthers the University's objective of excellence in research, scholarship, and education by publishing worldwide. Oxford is a registered trade mark of Oxford University Press in the UK and certain other countries.

Published in the United States of America by Oxford University Press 198 Madison Avenue, New York, NY 10016, United States of America.

© Steven G. Rogelberg 2019

Library of Congress Cataloging-in-Publication Data
Names: Rogelberg, Steven G., author.
Title: The surprising science of meetings: how you can lead your team to peak performance / Steven G. Rogelberg.
Description: New York: Oxford University Press, [2019] |
Includes bibliographical references and index.
Identifiers: LCCN 2018006496 | ISBN 9780190689216 (hardcover: alk. paper)
Subjects: LCSH: Business communication. | Meetings. | Leadership.
Classification: LCC HF5549.5.C6 R634 2018 | DDC 658.4/56—dc23
LC record available at https://lccn.loc.gov/2018006496

3 5 7 9 8 6 4 2

Printed by Sheridan Books, Inc., United States of America

Much love to Sandy, Sasha, and Gordon,
the three people I would go anywhere to meet with.

CONTENTS

Tools

PREFACE

Meetings are not in and of themselves problematic. Meetings are essential to teams and organizations. Without meetings, organizational democracy, inclusion, participation, buy-in, communication, attachment, teamwork, coordination, and cohesion would all be compromised. *What we need to rid ourselves of are bad meetings, wasted time in meetings, and unnecessary meetings.* This book is about solving these problems.

Meetings consume massive amounts of individual and organizational time, with a recent estimate suggesting there are fifty-five million meetings a day in the United States alone. The costs of this meeting time are staggering when weighted with the average salary data of attendees. It is estimated that the annual cost of meetings in the United States is a whopping $1.4 trillion—or 8.2 percent of the 2014 US GDP. Furthermore, this tremendous time investment yields only modest returns. "Too many meetings" was the number one time-waster at the office, cited by 47 percent of 3,164 workers in a study conducted by Salary.com focused on workplace time drains. Translating this into dollars, one reasonable estimate is that over $250 billion a year is wasted by having too many bad meetings. And these estimates do not include the indirect costs of bad meetings (e.g., employee frustration and strain).

Sadly, most companies and most leaders view poor meetings as inevitable because they don't know of better ways or they try new methods that don't stick, as they really are not founded in any scientific evidence of success. Also, bad meetings beget more bad meetings as dysfunctional practices become normative across the organization. Taken together, poor meetings become accepted as a way of life and a natural cost of doing business, like rain is a way of life in London. But, unlike the weather, meetings can indeed be improved.

Drawing on over fifteen years of original research I have conducted on the topic of meetings with my team, surveying and interviewing thousands of employees from hundreds of organizations, as well as drawing from a large number of evidence-based sources, my goal with this book is to translate the science of meetings to bring direction, guidance, and relief to those leading and participating in meetings. While many people I meet are surprised to hear that there are social and organizational scientists who study meetings, this research has produced large numbers of scientific publications, conference presentations, book chapters, dissertations, and extensive media coverage. And, of most relevance here, this science has produced insights and practical applications that can directly benefit executives and organizations by promoting efficiency, productivity, increased innovation and employee engagement, superior decisions, enhanced commitment to initiatives, better communication, and a greater sense of comradery across the workforce.

I wrote this book for any individual responsible for calling and leading meetings at work. This includes team leaders, supervisors, managers, directors, and senior executives across organizations and industry sectors. It is for learning and development professionals, executive coaches, and other educators who train and advise people on teamwork and leadership. It is for HR leaders and senior organizational leaders working to change the meeting culture at their organization.

Each chapter in this book goes into depth on a particular vexing meeting derailer as a way of setting up evidence-based solutions. As a general approach, I bring light to the types of dysfunctions at hand in meetings, and then provide a set of specific best practices and solutions to help you recover wasted time. I make these recommendations on the basis of reasonable extrapolations from the evidence, and also by examining what cutting-edge organizations like Google and Amazon are doing.

What counts as a meeting? Meeting sizes and meeting purposes can vary tremendously. In general, the focus here is on the most typical types of meetings found in organizations. They vary in size from two to fifteen attendees and generally are ostensibly about coordination, communication, decision-making, and monitoring. I cover everything here from the weekly meeting, to strategy meetings, to planning meetings, to task force meetings, to troubleshooting meetings, to brainstorming meetings, to debriefing meetings. That said, I can't imagine a meeting type or situation that would not benefit from learning about what works and what doesn't. Try applying what you learn here to a full-day retreat. Or to organizational training. Or to client meetings. Or to your community meeting, religious meeting, or PTA meeting. Every situation involving two or more people coming together for discussion, communication, coordination, or decision-making can benefit from a thoughtful evidence-based approach—an approach that truly honors the time and commitment of all parties.

Bad meetings can drain the life out of individuals and organizations. But meetings done well, leveraging evidence-based solutions like the ones we'll explore in this book, can be transformative and hugely positive. The cascading positive effects of improving just one meeting each day, across people and across time, yields not only tremendous organizational benefits—from cost savings to better organizational strategy—but also individual feelings of satisfaction, engagement, and accomplishment. At the same time, leaders and future leaders mastering meeting leadership skills are uniquely positioned to elevate their own career progression and personal success as they become highly adept at working with others, building relationships, unleashing others' full potential, and achieving team wins. Conversely, without these meeting leadership skills, one joins the ranks of so many others who bear the responsibility for the meeting "problem" and are the cause of so much frustration in the workplace.

Section I

SETTING THE MEETING STAGE

Chapter 1
SO MANY MEETINGS AND
SO MUCH FRUSTRATION

"I have way too many meetings."

Joe Nearly Everybody,
employee in Nearly Every Company, Inc.

Once I tell most anyone that I do research on meetings, I typically hear in response what I call the "meetings hell" lament. This lament usually includes comments such as (1) "All I do is sit in meetings"; (2) "If you want to know about bad meetings, follow me for a day"; (3) "We even have meetings on meetings"; or (4) "You need to study my organization, it is a case study for meeting dysfunction." Relatedly, popular press headlines abound expressing similar sentiments—take, for instance, the article in the *Harvard Business Review* titled "Stop the Meeting Madness." In fact, out of curiosity, I googled "too many meetings": there were over two hundred thousand hits.

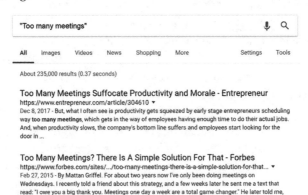

This raises the questions: How many meetings do people attend each day? Has that number increased over time? While the simple answers are "a lot" and "oh, yes," let's unpack those answers in a more diligent manner. First, to be able to count something, we have to define it. By defining what a meeting is, we can start tabulating the actual number of meetings that occur across the globe more systematically. With that, a *work meeting* is defined as a gathering of two or more employees for a purpose related to the functioning of an organization or a group (e.g., to direct, to inform, to govern, to regulate). The gathering can occur in a single modality (e.g., a video conference) or in a mixed-modality format (e.g., mostly face-to-face with one participant connected via telephone). Typically, meetings are scheduled in advance (some notice is provided) and are informally or formally facilitated by one of the attendees. Meetings can be extremely brief (five minutes) to a full day in length.

According to Elise Keith—cofounder of the software firm Lucid Meetings, who extrapolated information from the most commonly referenced meetings databases collected by Verizon, Microsoft, Fuze, and others—every day in the United States there are roughly fifty-five million workplace meetings. Yes, fifty-five million meetings *a day* in the United States alone. Forty plus years ago, in 1976, Antony Jay reported in the *Harvard Business Review* that there were approximately eleven million meetings per day in the country. Clearly, a massive increase in meetings has occurred over time.

Now let's take a look at how these massive numbers translate into the day-to-day experiences of individuals at work. Elise Keith's analysis, consistent with my research, suggests that non-managers attend eight meetings per week on average, while managers enjoy twelve meetings per week on average. These numbers would certainly be higher for particular job types (e.g., white-collar jobs), and meeting demands increase as we move up the organizational hierarchy, with those in the upper echelons of management spending most of their days booked solid with meetings. As for this level of managers, there is some intriguing work coming out of the Executive Time Use Project—a group of professors from the London School of Economics and Columbia and Harvard Universities studying how CEOs spend their time. In one study looking at 94 CEOs of top Italian firms and 357 corporate leaders in India, they found that 60 percent of CEOs' working hours and 56 percent of corporate leaders' working hours were spent in meetings, and these figures did not include conference calls!

To help put these numbers in context, I asked a set of executives each to tell me about a typical "day in the life" as it relates to meetings. I started with two CEOs. The first, a chancellor of a leading state university, reported that in his typical day he had seven meetings totaling nearly five hours.

CHANCELLOR OF A STATE UNIVERSITY	
SEVEN MEETINGS TOTALING FOUR HOURS AND FORTY-FIVE MINUTES	
8:00–9:00 a.m.	Routine status meeting with direct report with chief of staff present
9:00–9:30 a.m.	Routine status meeting with direct report with chief of staff present
9:30–10:00 a.m.	Routine status meeting with direct report with chief of staff present
11:30 a.m.–12:00 p.m.	Phone meeting with two other leaders to discuss ADA issue
1:00–2:00 p.m.	Meeting with candidate for the oversight committee
2:00–3:00 p.m.	Rehearsal for new student convocation
3:15–3:30 p.m.	Meeting about the search for a new director of a center; three attendees total

The CEO of a large national advocacy nonprofit also provided me with a typical day. The day involved eight meetings lasting a total of six and a half hours.

CEO OF A NATIONAL ADVOCACY ORGANIZATION	
EIGHT MEETINGS TOTALING SIX HOURS AND THIRTY MINUTES	
9:30–11:00 a.m.	Meeting with Executive Leadership Team (ten people in this meeting)
11:00 a.m.–12:00 p.m.	Meeting with Counsel re: litigation (four people in this meeting)
12:00–12:30 p.m.	Meeting with CFO (two people in this meeting)
1:00–1:30 p.m.	Call with Executive Committee of External Board (seven people in this meeting)
1:30–2:00 p.m.	Meeting with SVP of Human Resources (two people in this meeting)
3:00–3:30 p.m.	Interview with iHeart Radio
4:00–5:00 p.m.	Meeting to discuss international communications strategy and fundraising (six people in this meeting)
5:30–6:30 p.m.	Meeting with a national journalist

Next, I discussed meeting load with a senior vice president and chief human resources officer at one of the largest global food and beverage companies in the world. The day she shared with me, which she indicated was typical, involved six and a half hours in meetings, with a number of her meetings on this particular day dedicated to preparing for a future meeting: an annual succession planning meeting with a sector CEO.

SENIOR VP OF A HUMAN RESOURCES AND TALENT MANAGEMENT AT A GLOBAL FOOD AND BEVERAGES COMPANY	
SIX MEETINGS TOTALING SIX HOURS AND THIRTY MINUTES	
8:00–9:00 a.m.	Meet with business leader and three direct reports to prepare for annual succession planning meeting with sector CEO
10:00–11:00 a.m.	Discussion meeting with two direct reports around strategy for an executive assessment program

11:00 a.m.– 12:00 p.m.	Meeting with another business leader to prepare for our succession planning meeting with our sector CEO (five people at this meeting)
1:00–2:00 p.m.	Meeting with five business leaders to make sure our slates are all aligned for our upcoming succession planning meeting with the sector CEO (six people at this meeting)
2:30–4:30 p.m.	People planning prep—meeting another business leader (SVP of Sales) to prepare for succession planning (four people in this meeting)
4:30–5:00 p.m.	External partner meeting—phone call with external strategic partner to discuss employee transition project (six people on this call)

Why Are There So Many Meetings?

Clearly, there is a great deal of meeting activity going on at work, especially for those toward the top of the organization. This again raises the question why are there so many meetings. Putting aside the fact that some leaders may overuse meetings given their personal proclivities (e.g., an unwillingness to make a decision; a desire to "appear" active to others), the answer to this question is multifaceted and in many ways reflects a changing societal and organizational zeitgeist around work. Beliefs around the value and benefits of employee inclusion, of empowerment, of teams, of employee buy-in, and of employee engagement are more prominent than ever as efficient ways to achieve short-term and long-term organizational survival and success. Meetings are a key mechanism to express these values.

Relatedly, democratization has penetrated deeply into organizational life, with "command and control" leadership models becoming less dominant. Instead, organizations have become flatter and less hierarchical. Again, all roads lead to more meetings—the mechanism to bring people together, gain input, promote discussion, promote synergy, provide voice, explain things, coordinate, foster ownership, and learn and grow as a unit. In the *Harvard Business Review* article mentioned at the start of this chapter, a senior executive from a pharmaceutical company noted:

> *I believe that our abundance of meetings at our company is the Cultural Tax we pay for the inclusive, learning environment that we want to foster . . . and I'm ok with that. If the alternative to more meetings is more autocratic decision-making, less input from all levels throughout the organization, and fewer opportunities to ensure alignment and communication by personal interaction, then give me more meetings any time!*

While in Chapter 2 I will argue that the elimination of meetings in and of themselves is absolutely a false goal—the goal should actually be to eliminate ineffective and bloated meetings—it is still important to take stock of what meetings are implicitly and explicitly costing an organization, and what the return is on that investment.

How Much Money Are We Investing in Meetings?

The most basic way of calculating meeting cost considers time and salaries. For each attendee, calculate the amount of time in the meeting multiplied by his or her hourly salary. Then, add each attendee's sum together. For example, say there is a director-level staff meeting with seven people that lasts an hour, with an average yearly salary of $120,000 per attendee (approximately $60 an hour). That meeting alone would cost $420. If this staff meeting occurs every week for a year, the total annual cost is about $21,000 for just that one meeting. Or, consider a more senior leadership cabinet meeting with twelve attendees, two hours in length, and an average attendee salary of $240,000 (approximately $120 an hour): each meeting would cost $2,880. If this happens once every two weeks, the overall cost for the year would be approximately $74,880. It is easy to see that as the number of meetings compounds across people, layers of management, and time, the costs become tremendously high. Now, let's extrapolate even further by viewing the issue from a corporate perspective. Xerox, for example, estimated the immediate costs of meetings in their twenty-four-thousand-person manufacturing and development unit. In terms of meeting time and employee pay, costs were estimated at $100.4 million annually. Other studies suggest that 15 percent of the personnel budget is spent on meeting time. Finally, going to a societal level, Elise Keith's analyses estimate the cost of meetings in the United States at $1.4 trillion spent per year—or 8.2 percent of the 2014 US GDP.

Interestingly, these figures are actually *underestimating* the costs of meetings. In addition to not using "fully loaded" salaries, which include employee-benefits costs, the estimations ignore the direct costs associated with the meeting space, meeting equipment, and potential travel costs of attendees. Furthermore, and perhaps most importantly, these estimates do not take into consideration indirect costs associated with *bad meetings*—meetings deemed a poor use of time by attendees. Indirect costs include opportunity costs: time that could be spent elsewhere productively, even if this is just quiet time to explore thoughts and generate new ideas (i.e., to just catch one's breath and stop to reflect and think). Then there are the potential psychological costs associated with employees suffering through bad meetings. This includes erosion of employee engagement, employee frustration, the draining of employee spirit, and time spent ruminating and grousing over bad meetings. Finally, there is the concept of "meeting recovery syndrome," which refers to the time spent winding down after a frustrating meeting. This recovery process not only affects the frustrated attendee but also potentially zaps the energy of those around the individual upon hearing the complaints and providing support.

When you take into account all the direct costs and potential indirect costs, the investment in meetings is incredibly significant. If you liken a meeting to a type of communication technology, could this actually be one of the largest unidentified line items in an organizational budget? I can say with confidence that there is no single investment of this magnitude that an organization makes that is treated in such a cavalier manner; where so few resources are allocated to assessing, evaluating, and working to improve meetings, both locally and enterprise-wide.

What Does the Science Say? Are Meetings Working? Are They an Effective Use of Time?

Scientific reports on meeting effectiveness vary a fair amount. On the one hand, there is extensive evidence that meetings are draining the life out of individuals, teams, and organizations. For example, in 2005, Microsoft surveyed close to forty thousand people about productivity and work-related practices. They found that 69 percent globally, and 71 percent of workers in the United States, indicated that meetings were not productive. Then, a 2012 survey conducted by Salary.com, regarding time-wasters at work, revealed that "too many meetings" was the number one time-waster at the office; in fact, 47 percent of the 3,164 workers reported this answer. Finally, in 2014, Harris Poll conducted a survey for Clarizen, a project management company, involving over two thousand working adults. The focus was on what they referred to as "status meetings," which are defined as meetings with updates for team members on completed and in-progress work activities. Nearly three of every five workers reported that they multitask during status meetings. Almost 50 percent of respondents indicated that they would rather do any unpleasant activity (e.g., go to the Department of Motor Vehicles) than attend a status meeting. Overall, 35 percent of respondents indicated that status meetings are a "waste of time."

These data certainly look bleak with regard to meetings. I can also say these data are quite consistent with what I observe when I speak to leaders at training sessions. Namely, often I will do an exercise with attendees, asking them as a group to give me some insight into the quality of their meetings. I tell them, "I want to know what percentage of your meetings are not a good use of time." I then name percentages and ask them to clap if the percentage stated aligns with their experiences. Almost unequivocally, "50 to 70 percent of meetings are a waste of time" receives the most applause, regardless of whether I ask this question of an audience in South America, Asia, Europe, or North America.

Now, with all this said, there are some data suggesting the evaluations of meetings are not as depressing. Verizon surveyed over a thousand "heavy meeting goers." When participants were asked about meeting productivity, the results were more favorable than earlier data shared:

22% indicated their meetings were extremely productive
44% indicated their meetings were very productive
27% indicated their meetings were somewhat productive
6% indicated their meetings were not very productive
1% indicated their meetings were not at all productive

And in a study I conducted with over a thousand employees and managers, I asked participants to evaluate the quality of their meetings in general. The results were fairly similar to those of Verizon's study:

17% rated their meetings as very good to excellent
42% rated their meetings as good
25% rated their meetings as neither good nor bad
15% rated their meetings as poor or very poor

So, What Is the Truth?

Taken together, the "truth" is likely an average of all the data just presented, which would result in a generally negative assessment of meetings, but with a good number of useful meeting experiences thrown in (likely tied to certain leaders who truly are good at running meetings). However, even if you fully identify with the somewhat more positive meeting data presented here, it is still obvious that (1) there is much room for improvement in meetings, and (2) there is a ton of frustration being expressed. Relatedly, the research on meetings is certainly clear about the existence of a wide range of problems that we must work to overcome (e.g., the meeting being dominated by one or two people). That said, the most important truth is your own local truth—what truly matters most is your organization's return on its meeting investment. To help you identify the truth for your team, your department, and your organization, I have provided here a meeting-quality self-assessment.

Self-Assessment: Are You Maximizing Your Return on Investment from Your Meetings?

At the end of the book, a variety of tools are provided to help you better understand your meeting experiences and, most importantly, to improve them. One tool is called the "Meeting Quality Assessment—Calculation of a Wasted Meeting Time Index." In this tool you are asked to indicate the percentage of time that certain "negative things" happen or are present in your meetings. This assessment covers the following:

1. Meeting design
2. The meeting itself: time dynamics
3. The meeting itself: interpersonal dynamics
4. The meeting itself: discussion dynamics
5. Post-meeting

A scoring metric is then provided. The grand average percent that is calculated represents *wasted meeting investment*. In other words, this grand average is a wasted-time index. Here is a guide to interpret your grand scores, based on my work with organizations:

- If your scores are between 0 and 20 percent wasted meeting investment, your meetings are really quite productive. While there is room for improvement, your scores are above what is typical.

- If your scores are between 21 and 40 percent wasted meeting investment, your meetings are generally hit or miss. Plenty of time is being wasted. Improvements need to be made, but your scores are (sadly) typical of what we find in organizations.
- If your scores are above 41 percent wasted meeting investment, your meetings need substantial improvement. Your scores are considerably below average.

Taken together, the data are clear that meetings are a ubiquitous activity filling calendars and days. We can easily argue that meetings are accounting for years of time in one's professional work life. In considering typical evaluations of meeting quality and the return on meeting investment, we should be highly motivated to solve the problems with meetings. In the next chapter we queue up a path forward.

Takeaways

1. The amount of time we are spending in meetings is increasing, especially when we look at those involving upper management. Although the statistics vary, it is important to realize that meetings take up an increasingly large amount of time in employees' days.
2. The amount of time spent in meetings translates into big money for today's companies—at the societal level, one estimate comes in at a cost of $1.4 trillion. These costs are underestimates, as they do not include opportunity costs and employee frustration.
3. Although there is evidence to suggest that meetings are a waste of time and are negative experiences for employees, there are also data to suggest that meetings can be productive and meaningful. This provides hope that we can truly solve the meeting problem.
4. Take the time to do the Meeting Quality Self-Assessment, provided at the end of the book, to assess your meetings' return on investment. It's important to do this self-assessment from time to time to ensure that your meetings are positive and productive (and encourage your coworkers to do the same)—remember, your organization has a meeting culture that reflects how everyone runs meetings.

Chapter 2
GET RID OF MEETINGS?
NO, SOLVE MEETINGS
THROUGH SCIENCE

A *roast* is an event where a particular person is subjected to an avalanche of jokes, at his or her expense, to entertain the broader audience. Let's imagine for a moment that the particular person roasted is not a person but instead a thing: MEETINGS. It would not be difficult to roast the concept of meetings. Leveraging quotes from journalists or authors (e.g., George Will), economists (e.g., John Kenneth Galbraith), and a host of anonymous sources, the routine might sound something like this:

"If you had to identify, in one word, the reason why the human race has not achieved, and never will achieve, its full potential, that word would be *meetings*."

"A *meeting* is an event where minutes are taken and hours wasted."

"We will continue having meetings until we find out why no work is getting done."

"If I die, I hope it's during a staff meeting because the transition to death would be so subtle."

"I'm pretty sure the dinosaurs died out when they stopped gathering food and started having meetings to discuss gathering food."

"Meetings are indispensable when you don't want to do anything."

"Our meetings are held to discuss many problems that would never arise if we held fewer meetings."

"Football incorporates the two worst elements of American society: violence punctuated by committee meetings."

Would eliminating meetings make the world a better place? Was the great management guru Peter Drucker correct when he said, "Meetings are a symptom of bad organization. The fewer meetings the better"? The answer is an emphatic "no." The solution is not to dramatically reduce or eliminate meetings (although occasionally reducing meetings is reasonable and appropriate when there is no compelling purpose to meet). Abolishing meetings is a false solution. Schedules with too few meetings are associated with substantial risks for employees, leaders, teams, and organizations. In this chapter, we will look at the evidence for why it is inadvisable to stamp out meetings. Following this, I will try to convince you that the genuine solution to excessive bad meetings is applying the science of meetings to fix them.

We Need to Meet, and We Need to Meet Critical Needs

Not holding enough meaningful meetings will likely derail employees, leaders, teams, and organizations. Holding too few meetings robs employees of essential information and feelings of inclusion, support, voice, and community. Meetings help employees build attachments to others and recognize that they are not alone in silos but instead are part of something bigger than themselves. Meetings make it possible for individual attendees to connect in a highly human way, serving to build relationships, networks, and, most important, support. Meetings serve as vehicles to efficiently bring together ideas, thoughts, and opinions and should enable each person to perform his or her job in a better, more coordinated and co-operative way. Meetings help both leaders and employees to better "make sense" of organizational life, challenges, ambiguities, and opportunities—to create a shared understanding that promotes efficiency and teamwork. Meetings foster commitment to goals and initiatives that connect jobs, as well as commitment to broader departmental and organizational aspirations that may not be explicitly stated in any individual job description. Meetings bring individuals together as a coherent whole. As a result, this coherent whole can be more adaptive, resilient, and self-directing, especially in the face of crisis.

Meetings can be stages for leaders to truly lead, share their visions, be authentic, and inspire and engage their team. At the same time, meetings are a form of localized democracy where ideas and innovation can emerge through employee interaction—even the smallest voices have the opportunity to be heard and to be given life and influence. Perhaps most importantly, meetings are sites for promoting consensus, thus serving as a focal point for collective drive and energy.

In so many ways, meetings are the building blocks and core elements of the organization: they are venues where the organization comes to life for employees, teams, and leaders. Finally, let's not forget that humans are inherently social creatures who crave interaction and belonging, not isolation. For instance, in some research I have done, employees were asked a simple question: "If you could design your ideal work day, what would it look like"? In these private and reflective surveys, respondents consistently advocated for meetings as part of their day. In fact, a day without meetings was not considered desirable.

Taking all this information together, it is clear that the elimination of meetings is a false solution. Instead, we must work to make meetings better. The meeting problem can indeed be "solved" through the application of meeting science, rather than with speculative wisdom. This evidence can break the cycle of bad meetings: meetings that beget more bad meetings as dysfunctional practices become normative across organizations.

A Brief Introduction to the Ways Scientists Study Meetings

Meeting science is the study of meetings themselves, including what goes on before, during, and after meetings. It examines meetings not only as a critical workplace phenomenon affecting individuals, leaders, and organizations, but also as a context or container of sorts to study groups, their processes, and their success or lack thereof. Hundreds of studies relevant to meetings exist examining a range of topics, from pre-meeting talk, to lateness, to meeting design, to meeting processes, to decision-making, to cohesion, to meeting success predictors. Although there has been an explosion of research on meetings in this past decade, historical work on team effectiveness from more than sixty years back connects readily to the topic at hand. Meeting science is conducted using a number of methodologies, including field survey studies, lab studies, and experimental research involving confederates. Let me share some exemplars to illustrate the different approaches used in meeting science to provide a better feel for just how the research is carried out. The findings from these studies—and so many others—will be used throughout the book to better inform meeting practices.

Field Survey Studies

In one of my first projects on meetings, we surveyed nearly a thousand managers and non-managers in the United States, the United Kingdom, and Australia. We used a daily and general field survey approach to answer the following research question: "How are employee job attitudes influenced by meetings and does this depend on the person, the nature of the job, and the nature of the meeting?" Participants completed either (1) a single end-of-day survey asking about their meetings and job attitudes that day, or (2) a general survey where they discussed their meetings overall and their job attitudes. In both surveys, we also collected demographic information about the respondents and their jobs.

Field survey studies can also be used to collect data over periods of time. Joe Allen, one of my former doctoral students and now a leading scholar on meetings, conducted a longitudinal-type field study of 319 working adults. He aimed to examine how their managers ran meetings at one point in time and employee engagement at another point in time to address the question, "How do managerial meeting leadership practices relate to an employee's overall job engagement?" Employee engagement is a highly desired outcome for organizations, given its relationship to employee performance, innovation, and even customer satisfaction.

The next two examples are of controlled laboratory studies done on the topic of meetings.

Laboratory/Experimental Studies

Allen Bluedorn and his colleagues conducted an intriguing experiment on stand-up meetings, a popular, relatively new form of employee meeting without seating. They used this laboratory study to answer the question, "How are meeting outcomes affected by conducting a meeting standing in comparison to sitting?" The researchers brought students into a lab setting to form five-person groups with the task of solving a problem. Groups were randomly assigned to one of two conditions: (1) a "sitting around a meeting table" condition (fifty-six groups), or (2) a "standing-up meeting" condition (fifty-five groups). The group's solution to the problem was scored. In order to address the research question, the researchers measured both the group's performance and the amount of time the group spent working.

Sometimes in an experimental study, a researcher uses a *confederate* (a person who appears to be involved as a participant but, unbeknownst to others, is part of the research team). Sigal Barsade, a professor at Yale University, employed a confederate to examine the concept of emotional contagion—the transference of mood states among meeting attendees—and how that affects actual meeting processes associated with success. The research question that drove this study was as follows: "How are individual moods and emotions in meetings affected by the confederate and, if there is contagion, how does that affect group cooperation, conflict, and perceived task performance?" Twenty-nine teams of business school undergraduates were formed; each attendee took on the role of a department head in a simulated leaderless group discussion. Included in the meeting was a confederate. The confederate conveyed either positive types of emotional behaviors (e.g., cheerfulness) or negative types of emotional behaviors (e.g., irritability) throughout the meeting. The researchers coded whether the emotion spread; group performance was assessed, and participants then answered a survey about how they were feeling to see if it matched the behaviors displayed by the confederate.

Interested in what these research studies found? Keep reading; the answers will be revealed later. In fact, throughout the book, insights from meeting science will be integrated with the ultimate goal of fully realizing the potential of meetings. Andy Grove, the former CEO of Intel, was passionate about seeking to improve meetings. He once wrote, "Just as you would not permit a fellow employee to steal a piece of office equipment worth $2,000, you shouldn't let anyone walk away with the time of his fellow managers." A poorly conducted and unnecessary meeting is indeed a form of time theft, a theft that can be prevented.

Takeaways

1. Although there is evidence that the number of meetings is increasing and there are plenty of bad meetings, doing away with meetings is not a good or viable alternative. Meetings help employees connect, voice their opinions, tackle problems, and create a shared understanding.

2. Instead of eliminating meetings, we need to improve them using what we know from meeting science, which is the study of

meetings themselves and everything and everyone involved in meetings.

3. Meeting science can take many forms—from general one-time or daily surveys, to longitudinal surveys and even laboratory studies. These different, yet complementary approaches help researchers answer questions and generate knowledge about different aspects of meetings.

Section II

EVIDENCE-BASED STRATEGIES FOR LEADERS

Chapter 3
THE IMAGE IN THE MIRROR IS LIKELY WRONG

"Self-awareness gives you the capacity to learn from your mistakes as well as your successes. It enables you to keep growing."

Larry Bossidy,
former chairman and CEO of AlliedSignal

"If you lack self-awareness you can't change. Why should you? As far as you're concerned you're doing everything right."

Jim Whitt,
author and founder, Purpose Unlimited

There is compelling evidence suggesting that we are poor judges of our own leadership skills when it comes to meetings. Namely, we have an inflated view of our skills. This inflated perception, in turn, results in a sizable blind spot that likely prevents us from developing, improving, honing, and maximizing our ability to lead meetings. Given how essential meeting leadership is, the "victims" in this narrative are the meeting attendees themselves; they are the ones who experience the consequences of unproductive leadership practices. Furthermore, these unproductive practices have the potential to become the norm across the organization ("this is just how we do things") and consequently spread to other managers and their meetings, infect new leaders, and ultimately define the meeting culture of the organization. In other words, we must not ignore the risk that poor meeting leadership skills will beget poor meeting leadership skills in others.

In this chapter, I will share how I reached these conclusions about our misaligned self-perceptions. Then I will discuss what we can do to promote accurate self-awareness of our meeting skills—to align the image in the mirror with reality. And, perhaps most importantly, we will discuss the target image in the mirror: the image leaders should aspire to see.

Human Bias in How We Perceive Ourselves

A Prairie Home Companion was a live radio program introduced in 1974 on Minnesota Public Radio. The show was set in Lake Wobegon, a fictional town. The town was described as a place where "all the women are strong, all the men are good looking, and all the children are above average." From this, psychology professor David Myers coined the term the "Lake Wobegon Effect," which refers to the robust human tendency to overestimate—relative to others—one's knowledge, skills, abilities, and personality traits. In other words, most people believe they are well above average, which clearly is a statistical impossibility.

One of the first studies on this effect was conducted by researchers at the College Board, the publisher of the SAT exam. They attached a research survey to the SAT exam asking students to provide self-ratings on a variety of personal characteristics, such as leadership and the ability to get along well with others. Seventy percent of the students rated themselves as being above the median on leadership. With regard to the ability to get along well with others, 85 percent indicated they were above the median, and a whopping 25 percent indicated they were in the top 1 percent!

One reaction to these data is to assume that this is just another example of the warped and narcissistic teenage mindset and that these results would not extend to more grounded adults. Well, not so fast. Faculty at the University of Nebraska were surveyed about their teaching ability. Over 90 percent rated themselves as above average, and 68 percent indicated that they were in the top 25 percent. Another research project looked at self-perceptions of driving skills relative to others'. When asked about driving safety, 88 percent of a US sample indicated they were in the top 50 percent of drivers. Most recently, a unique study was conducted with prisoners in England, the majority of whom had been convicted of either violence against people or robbery. The participants were asked to compare their standing, relative to other prisoners and non-prisoners, on nine traits, such as kindness, generosity, self-control, morality, and law-abidingness. In light of the other results presented here, it should come as no surprise that the vast majority of participants rated themselves as "better than the average inmate" on all traits. What is most interesting is that when the inmates compared themselves to non-prisoners, they still rated themselves as better on all dimensions, with one exception: they rated themselves as equal to non-prisoners on law-abidingness. For our international readers who may think this does not apply in their country, research has found this "better-than-average bias" in diverse sets of samples from Germany, Israel, Sweden, Japan, and Australia.

Focusing Back on Meeting Leadership

Although direct tests of the self-inflation bias with regard to meetings do not yet exist, a host of related evidence paints a not-so-rosy picture. In multiple studies my colleagues and I conducted, we found that meeting leaders consistently rated their meetings more favorably than non-leaders. Thus, a leader's experience of the meeting appears to be fundamentally different from the experiences of other meeting attendees, with leaders thinking things were, well, quite glorious. Additional research provides some insight into this finding. For example, in a study I conducted with Sophie Tong, a professor from Peking University, we found that the amount of participation or involvement in meetings correlated positively with perceptions of meeting effectiveness and satisfaction. In other words, if you talk a lot, you are more likely to think the meeting experience was a good one. Well, guess who typically talks the most in meetings? The leader.

Finally, referring back to the Verizon telephone survey of more than thirteen hundred meeting-goers that was mentioned in Chapter 1, as you may expect, respondents rated the meetings they themselves initiated as being extremely or very productive (79 percent). Meetings initiated by peers, in contrast, were evaluated as being significantly lower in productivity, with 56 percent of the meetings seen as extremely or very productive.

Taken together, leaders seem to have an overly positive sense of the meeting experience compared to that of meeting attendees. This inflated optimism ultimately diminishes self-awareness and the ability to truly recognize one's own developmental needs. Hence, the premise of this chapter: the leader's image in the meeting mirror is likely wrong.

What an Organization Can Do to Improve Leader Self-Awareness

The path to meeting enlightenment is multipronged. Before talking extensively about what each leader can personally do, it is important to recognize that organizations themselves can develop systems and practices that promote self-awareness (and accountability) among their leaders more broadly. These systems and practices take a few different forms. First and foremost, to facilitate self-awareness, leaders need meaningful meeting skills and facilitation training. After all, if you don't truly know what excellent meeting behaviors look like, you don't have an internal standard of sorts to compare yourself to. This type of training is essential, especially as it is rare to see this content domain addressed in bachelor's-level business programs, standard MBA programs, or on-boarding programs, let alone among the millions of liberal arts graduates who enter the workforce. Andy Grove was arguably one of the greatest CEOs in modern history and was so passionate about the importance of meetings that he required every new employee—literally everyone, regardless of position—to take Intel's course on effective meetings. He was so devoted to this ideal that, for many years, he actually taught the course himself.

The second major prong to promoting self-awareness is feedback. A company's annual employee engagement and attitude survey must contain content on meetings in order to provide data on how leaders are doing. To date, I have identified only a couple of Fortune 500 companies engaged in this practice. This really is unfathomable—how could a frequent organizational activity like meetings not be a topic on these surveys? Without such content, organizations and, more importantly, individual leaders are left in the dark about whether their meetings are working as well as they think they are. In turn, they remain blind to employee suggestions on how to improve meetings.

Another opportunity for leader development and accountability is to conduct 360-degree feedback surveys that contain some content on meetings. With 360-degree feedback, a leader receives aggregated anonymous feedback from key groups of individuals: their peers, their direct reports, and their boss. Typically, organizations outsource 360-degree survey efforts to consulting companies. I have yet to find one consulting company that includes any content around meetings in its assessment. Given the amount of time spent in meetings, it is hard to imagine a bigger oversight in our leadership development toolbox. To facilitate these feedback efforts, I have provided sample engagement survey questions and sample 360-degree feedback questions in the "Tools" section at the end of this book.

Taken together, when it comes to organizational practices to promote feedback about meetings to leaders and accountability for being a poor meeting leader, we are in the dark ages. However, it is not *all* doom and gloom—there are some nice examples of innovative meeting evaluation practices in certain companies. Take, for instance, efforts exercised by Weight Watchers at their New York headquarters. They installed touchscreen tablets outside their conference rooms to capture anonymous feedback about the meetings just completed there. They keep the feedback quite simple: meeting attendees rate the last meeting on a five-point meeting-quality scale using emojis. Weight Watchers leverages the ratings to identify if interventions are needed and to ultimately assess the effectiveness of interventions attempted. For example, after installing agenda whiteboards—one of the suggested interventions—meeting dissatisfaction dropped from 44 percent to 16 percent. That said, perhaps the biggest value of an initiative such as this is actually more subtle in nature. By engaging in this practice of rating meetings and making improvements based on feedback, Weight Watchers is creating a culture that elevates the importance of meetings.

How Can Leaders Take Control of Their Meeting Leadership Skill Development?

When I'm working with executives and managers who want to make their meetings more effective, I recommend that they start by truly "seeing" their own meetings. Specifically, there are signals that, if we look carefully, inform us about meeting leadership abilities.

- If attendees are on their phones throughout the meeting multitasking, that is likely a negative reflection on our leadership.
- If attendees are engaging in a host of side conversations, that is a negative reflection on our leadership.
- If we are doing most, if not all, of the talking, that is indeed a negative reflection on our leadership.
- If one or two attendees are dominating the meeting discussion, it likely suggests that we did not construct an agenda highly relevant to all, that we have not created a psychologically "safe" setting in which folks can engage,

or that we are not actively facilitating the meeting—all of which are not a positive reflection on our leadership.

These signals serve as feedback. If they are present for you, it's time to consider some change.

Putting this informal scanning of cues aside, the best practice for you, as a leader, is to evaluate your standing meetings every three months or so. The evaluation should be quick and easy: a survey given to all attendees containing just a handful of questions. Let me share with you an assessment with some results collected from RSC Bio Solutions, located in Charlotte, North Carolina. The CEO implemented daily fifteen-minute meetings (aka *huddles*) with his commercial team to improve communication and coordination. A couple of months later, he administered the following short assessment to evaluate the huddles, shared here along with the annotated results.

COMMERCIAL HUDDLE CHECK-IN SURVEY

OCTOBER 18, 2016, 7:25 A.M. EDT

Q1: Overall, how useful are our Commercial huddles to you?

Answer	%	Count
Very useful	42.86%	3
Moderately useful	57.14%	4
Somewhat useful	0.00%	0
A little useful	0.00%	0
Not useful	0.00%	0

Q2: With regard to promoting communication, teamwork, and coordination, how effective do you feel our Commercial huddles are overall?

Answer	%	Count
Very effective	57.14%	4
Moderately effective	28.57%	2
Somewhat effective	14.29%	1
A little effective	0.00%	0
Not effective at all	0.00%	0

Q3: Overall, are you glad we are having Commercial huddles?		
Answer	%	Count
Yes	100.00%	7
No	0.00%	0

Q4: What do you think is working well about the Commercial huddles?
"Cross-communication and awareness have been good; much more cooperative effort, prompts action."
"Collaboration and overall better communications throughout the Commercial team."
"Delivers a level of accountability and brings up areas where teamwork can be effective."
"Keeping everyone in the loop and feeling part of a team. Keep moving things forward."
"Sense of urgency is increasing. I see the huddles initiating collaborative work outside the huddle that wouldn't otherwise happen. People are made aware of key things faster. We are removing obstacles as a result."

Q5: What do you think we can do better/differently to make our Commercial huddles more effective?
"Continue to remind people to focus on key items and roadblocks. Still get into the weeds too often."
"1. Everyone must stay focused and concise (60–90 sec) for daily report-out— i.e., Roadblocks; Wins or Movement; Top Priority for the day. This would leave more time for questions/clarifications, suggestions/tips, and BRIEF beneficial discussion. *2. Every other day vs. every day?"*
"I find that daily huddles can be somewhat distracting, it seems that mornings tend to be my most productive time. I suggest trying two or three times a week versus daily. I think we'd have the same results."
"Less about all of the tasks . . . more focus on bigger issues and opportunities. Would love to see us sharing more wins/successes/accomplishments."

The CEO was pleased that the huddles were well received and that folks derived value, but he acknowledged there were opportunities for improvement. Instead of reducing the frequency of the huddles as some suggested, he wanted to first see if they could make adjustments to the meetings to increase quality. He noted that a number of comments alluded to feelings of monotony and a lack of tightness around conversation. To address these concerns, he created additional huddle discussion prompts to try periodically. They also started rotating huddle leadership responsibilities and encouraged daily leaders to experiment with new prompts to spark energy and important insights. Before some meetings, he reminded folks what to avoid during huddles: just a long accounting of day-to-day activity (this serves to set expectations). After another assessment, they will see what effect these changes have had and then determine if it is best for the frequency of huddles to decrease.

You can adapt this survey for your own meetings or just go with a very basic, three-question stop, start, and continue survey:

1. What am I not doing so well as the meeting leader (need to stop doing)?
2. What should I start doing that I am not currently doing?
3. What am I doing well as the meeting leader (need to keep doing)?

A survey such as this can be administered using an anonymous online survey platform (e.g., a free Qualtrics or SurveyMonkey account). The survey directions provided to participants are key. Here is an example:

I want to be the best possible leader I can be. I want our meetings to use time effectively. To achieve these goals, I need your candid feedback. Please answer the following questions as honestly as possible. I will summarize the overall themes in the results, report out to all, implement actions to promote positive change, and then resurvey down the road to see if it helped.

Instructions like these serve to reinforce a climate of excellence, of continual learning, and of inclusiveness. Notice that I recommend reporting findings to the team as part of those directions—this is key, too. After others take the survey and you have compiled the data, summarize the major themes and specific actions you are going to take moving forward. Share your observations at a future meeting or via email.

Ultimately, meaningful evaluations of meetings and meeting leadership start to align what we see in the mirror with reality. This raises the next critical question: what image should we aspire to see in the mirror?

What Image Do You Want to See?

The image you want to see—that is, the type of meeting leader you want to aspire to be—is one closely aligned with servant leadership. By elevating and helping others, a servant leader experiences success for him- or herself, for others, and for the organization. This type of person makes the needs of others a priority and works to meet them and, more broadly, aims to help others grow. By doing so, others maximize their potential and abilities, and they feel "safe" fully engaging at work. As a result, the promise of a team and a meeting is more readily realized as the collective talent is unleashed. This latter point is key, as leveraging the knowledge, skills, and abilities of the attendees is often a main reason for creating teams and assembling people together. This is in sharp contrast to an egocentric, "leader-first" leadership approach, designed to elevate leaders themselves, drive the accumulation of power, and use that power for self-centered gain. The servant leader is comfortable sharing power and derives satisfaction and success when others prosper and the organization thrives. This type of leadership approach is a core part of the values and development process at many of the most successful global organizations. For example, it is the core leadership paradigm at SAS, The Container Store, Whole Foods, Zappos, and Starbucks.

This servant leadership style is highly consistent with the research described by Wharton professor Adam Grant in his book *Give and Take*. Grant discusses how employees make daily decisions on whether to act like givers or takers. Unlike takers, givers actively assist others and share knowledge— they do this without seeking a quid pro quo arrangement. The giving is done because it is just the "right" thing to do.

Research suggests that organizations in which giving is the norm among employees experience robust business outcomes around profitability, productivity, efficiency, employee satisfaction, and customer satisfaction. The question for us is how to apply what we know about servant leadership and a giver mindset to running effective meetings.

A leader with a servant-and-giver mindset recognizes his or her unique responsibility to make the meeting a good use of time. The meeting is not about the leader personally feeling the meeting had value; rather, it is about deriving value more broadly. Such leaders recognize that, as leaders, they must truly own others' experiences of the meeting. They think carefully about the design and execution of the meeting, from soup to nuts—they never just "phone it in." Instead, they plan and design the meeting experience they are orchestrating. This planning could take just a few minutes, but it is a sincere premeeting reflection on the agenda, the goals, the order of topics, potential problems, dynamics, and useful strategies to try. It further includes creating a psychologically safe environment where people can share genuine comments, concerns, and feedback.

Let me illustrate one potential manifestation of this mindset in action. True story: A highly respected leader created an implicit rule for himself in some discussion and decision-making meetings where folks tended to defer to him; he restricted his comments to just one or two sentences and, when possible, held back until discussion among attendees had occurred. The aim of this approach was to ensure that participants' thinking could evolve and that his comments wouldn't prematurely influence the discussion. This simple rule is very significant. Yes, it is quite extreme and not always practical, and this particular (servant) leader used this technique only when it fit the situation at hand. But engaging in a servant leader action like this led to rich, engaging, inclusive, and unexpected conversations. Overall, leaders like this are focused on meeting dynamics; they truly are keyed in on facilitating a good meeting experience, rather than elevating and promoting themselves. Being plugged in to managing group dynamics is, after all, the leader's role, as others will find it difficult to jump in to do this type of task given that it is not the norm for them to do so.

Some of the facilitation behaviors aligned with servant leadership are listed next. These are sample facilitation behaviors; a complete list can be found in the Good Meeting Facilitation Checklist in the "Tools" section at the end of the book.

Time Management

- Keeps track of time and paces the meeting effectively, given the big picture of the agenda.
- Does not rush through an emergent issue that truly needs to be discussed. Able to recognize if an issue raised would be best addressed at a subsequent meeting.
- Keeps conversation flowing (e.g., recognizing a tangent and pulling it back in to what needs to be discussed).

Active Listening

- Keeps clarifying and summarizing where things are and collects people's input so that everyone understands the process and the discussion at hand.
- Listens carefully for underlying concerns and helps bring them out so that they can be dealt with constructively.
- Keeps engaged with the note-taker so that issues, actions, and takeaways are recorded and not lost. Confirms with attendees that all is correct.

Conflict Management

- Encourages conflict around ideas (e.g., "any concerns with this idea"), and then actively embraces and manages the conflict so that positive benefits for performance and decision-making ensue.
- Maintains an environment where people are comfortable disagreeing (e.g., thanks people for sharing divergent points of view). Invites debate.

- Deals with disrespectful behavior quickly through re-direction, comments around staying constructive, and reminds attendees of the meeting ground rules.

Ensuring Active Participation

- Actively draws out input from others. Keeps mental track of who wants to speak and comes back to them.
- To keep an attendee from dominating the conversation, uses body language (e.g., a subtle and small hand movement to indicate the need to stop speaking) and transition statements (e.g., "thank you for that").
- Keeps side conversations at bay by reigning folks in when they lose focus.

Pushing for Consensus

- Tests for agreement and consensus to get a sense of where attendees are at, but does not unduly and unnecessarily pressure others to reach a conclusion when not ready (unless there is a time urgency).
- Knows when to intervene assertively in the meeting process and provide direction (e.g., the group lacks focus and is talking over one another) and when to let the process run as it is.
- Is an honest broker of the conversation at hand and does not privilege his or her viewpoint or ideas in the discussion. Works to remain impartial. Makes it clear that his or her opinion is just one opinion to be discussed.

Although these facilitation techniques are consistent with servant leadership and can certainly promote meeting success, *none of this precludes a leader from being direct and assertive and moving the discussion forward actively* if needed. In fact, jumping into the meeting fray and taking control might be exactly what is needed from the meeting leader. Or, it may be the case that the leader truly is the subject-matter expert at hand and being firm with her or his input is critical to success. With a servant-and-giver leader approach, however, this action is experienced as more genuine by the attendees who have experienced the leader's track record of inclusion and support.

Overall, servant-and-giver meeting leaders take pride in being excellent stewards of others' time and recognize that this is the path to their ultimate success, the success of others, and the success of the organization. This is a giver mindset. This is a servant leader mindset. This is the image you want to see in the mirror. And, ultimately, it leads to personal happiness. Namely, research regarding giving behaviors suggests that one of the most robust predictors of life satisfaction is helping others.

A great quote by author William Arthur Ward captures this theme well:

> *The adventure of life is to learn. The purpose of life is to grow. The nature of life is to change. The challenge of life is to overcome. The essence of life is to care. The opportunity of life is to serve. The secret of life is to dare. The spice of life is to befriend. The beauty of life is to give.*

Putting It All Together

In this chapter, I discussed why meeting leadership that we see every day may not be optimal, most notably how leaders' perceptions of their skills appear to be overinflated and exaggerated. Leaders are just not as skilled as they often think they are. This problem is left unchecked because of inadequate assessment of the meetings themselves and of those who lead them.

A study by Green Peak Partners and Cornell's School of Industrial and Labor Relations examined leader success among seventy-two executives at public and private companies. The conclusion was that high self-awareness was an exceptional predictor of overall success. Those with high self-awareness did a better job hiring subordinates and, perhaps most importantly, leveraging the talent around them. The tools in this chapter can help you gain more self-awareness, which, with training, the right mindset, trial, error, and more feedback, will improve the way you work with your team and lead meetings.

Takeaways

1. Realize—and embrace—the fact that you are likely not quite as good at leading meetings as you think you are. Evidence shows that we are likely to overestimate our abilities; accepting this reality is key to self-awareness and making improvements.
2. Given that we are likely to overestimate our abilities, take a pulse of your meeting leadership. How do others act in meetings? Are there side conversations? Are people on their phones? Have you tried administering a quick survey? Data like these will increase your self-awareness and give you more of an accurate picture than your perceptions alone.
3. Make increasing meeting leadership an organizational priority: start by suggesting that meetings be part of your 360-degree feedback for leaders; add a section to your yearly employee engagement survey on meetings. Do not try to make these improvements all on your own—make it a focus for everyone in order to create positive organizational change.
4. Try to adopt a servant leadership and giver mindset in order to unleash collective talent in a meeting and to foster buy-in. Ultimately, servant leadership will serve you well in and outside of meetings.

Chapter 4
MEET FOR FORTY-EIGHT MINUTES

Cultural norms abound. They influence how we think, how we speak, what we do, how we engage with others, even how we raise our children. Take, for instance, the concept of the tooth fairy. While many cultures do not have such a concept, in France, Spain, and Colombia, the tooth fairy is a mouse. In Greece, the child throws the tooth on the roof of the house instead of putting it under the pillow—this brings good luck and strong teeth. In Turkey, the parent buries the tooth near a location of meaning or future hopes (e.g., if the parents want their child to be a professor, they might bury the tooth near a university). In Russia, the child will often place the lost tooth in mouse holes. The mouse, in turn, will give the child a strong tooth as a replacement. In Malaysia, children bury their baby teeth, as they believe that teeth, being part of their body, should be returned to the earth. In looking at these various traditions, it is clear that what becomes the status quo for tens of millions of people within a country may be considered odd, perhaps even downright bizarre, by those outside the country.

In the way that organizations work, and with meetings in particular, there are a number of examples of this cultural diversity. In the Middle East and Latin America, for example, it is not at all unusual to start meetings nearly an hour late. Or, consider the length of meetings: the majority of workplace meetings are exactly one hour long. Think about this for a moment: despite the fact that meetings vary greatly in purpose, scope, history, communication modality, and the number of attendees, they often are exactly one hour in length, and the sixty-minute meeting has been a cultural norm for decades. In fact, it is such an accepted norm that when calendar software programs like Microsoft Outlook were developed, sixty minutes was the default setting when a meeting was scheduled. The norm begets the software default, and the default software setting reinforces the norm. In this chapter, we will explore the concept of meeting length, why the sixty-minute norm can be counterproductive, and some alternative approaches to the standard meeting length. Namely, I will discuss a set of practical recommendations given the pernicious effects of Parkinson's law.

Have Time, Will Fill It

In 1955, *The Economist* published a humorous essay titled "Parkinson's Law." The first paragraph reads as follows:

> *It is a commonplace observation that work expands so as to fill the time available for its completion. Thus, an elderly lady of leisure can spend the entire day in writing and despatching [sic] a postcard to her niece at Bognor Regis. An hour will be spent in finding the postcard, another in hunting for spectacles, half-an-hour in a search for the address, an hour and a quarter in composition, and twenty minutes in deciding whether or not to take an umbrella when going to the pillar-box in the next street. The total effort which would occupy a busy man for three minutes all told may in this fashion leave another person prostrate after a day of doubt, anxiety and toil.*

This notion of work expanding to fill time voids prompted much research—most of which provided empirical support for the concept.

Parkinson's law has been documented in many populations. In a classic study, management researchers Judith Bryan and Ed Locke conducted an experiment in which college students were asked to complete a fixed set of very simple arithmetic problems. Sounds easy enough, but here is the rub: some participants were assigned to an "excess time" condition and others were put in a condition where they had just the "right" amount of time for the problems at hand. Lo and behold, those in the excess time condition took significantly longer to complete the problems; it appeared that the students who had more time than they needed expended less effort and felt less urgency to complete their tasks expediently— Parkinson's law in action! Similar sets of findings have been found in other populations, from pulp mill workers to NASA scientists.

Parkinson's law manifests in non-time related ways as well. An intriguing study published in the *Journal of Criminal Justice* examined jail capacity and incarceration. It found that a large increase in jail capacity in Orange County, Florida, led to an increase in daily incarceration levels beyond what would be expected on the basis of police activity and preexisting incarceration. Stated differently, if we have space, we fill it. As humans, we seem to consciously or unconsciously strive to fill voids. This applies to meetings as well. If the meeting is scheduled for sixty minutes, it will generally take sixty minutes. John Morris, cartoonist for fifty-two years for the Associated Press, illustrated this in poignant fashion. In one published cartoon a conference table is surrounded by a set of meeting attendees with blank stares on their faces. The meeting leader exclaims, "There's no way we can come to a decision yet—this meeting has only lasted thirty minutes."

The fact that the work of a meeting generally expands to fill whatever amount of time you allot presents us with an opportunity. How much time can you reclaim for yourself and your coworkers by trimming and pruning your calendars? In the rest of this chapter, we will look at ways to more effectively set a meeting time so that it not only fits the task at hand but also creates reasonable pressure and poses a challenge the meeting attendees can rise up to. Finally, I will provide exemplars and discuss how companies can have super-speedy meetings without sacrificing effectiveness. Ultimately, decreasing a meeting's length not only returns time to the attendees but also creates a positive form of pressure, in turn sharpening attendees' focus and interest.

Decreasing Meeting Times Thoughtfully

John Watson, founder of IBM, posted a simple slogan through-out company offices that read: "Think." This simple rule of thumb can have endless applications for managers. One of these applications is in the determining of meeting times: with a given set of meeting goals, how much time is really needed to complete them? A meeting leader should take a minute to think and make an informed guess based on some key factors: the nature of the meeting's goals, the people invited to the meeting (discussed in a later chapter), and an analysis of past meetings. The same leader can also, at times, ask others for input and thoughtfully use that feedback, which only serves to engender attendee buy-in to time limits once they have been established. After considering these variables, don't be wary of scheduling meetings with odd lengths. For example, a forty-eight-minute meeting is just fine if that is the right fit. These odd times attract attention and curiosity and may even be a little fun. The survey research company TINYpulse, for example, starts a daily staff meeting at 8:48 a.m. Not only does this practice raise eyebrows because of its uniqueness, but also, as an added bonus, TINYpulse reports almost zero tardiness to these meetings.

Once a good time estimate is generated, consider dropping it by 5–10 percent. A little bit of pressure can often serve a meeting well. The Yerkes–Dodson law, which maps the relationship between stress and performance, is well established in psychological research. This relationship is one of an inverted U.

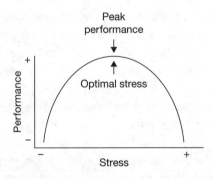

Namely, performance is optimal when some level of stress exists, and performance is lowest in the absence of stress, as well as when there is an abundance of stress. This pattern of findings exists for both individual and team performance, across both work and sports contexts. So, by dropping 5–10 percent off the well-considered estimate, you are potentially introducing a healthy amount of stress, which promotes task-related focus, stimulation, energy, and engagement. If you typically have a sixty-minute meeting, push it down to fifty minutes if that seems doable. If you typically have a thirty-minute meeting, push it down to twenty-five minutes. This clearly works to counter some of the negative effects of Parkinson's law. Plus it saves time, which compounds across participants. Finally, slightly decreasing meeting length has an added benefit of helping with transitions between meetings.

As we saw in Chapter 1, it is not atypical to have back-to-back meetings. Without any type of transition time, the chance of meeting lateness increases. My colleagues and I have conducted a host of studies on meeting lateness and we've learned that meetings seem to start late around 50 percent of the time. Meeting lateness by and large leads to frustration among those who are not late. Most worrisome, this frustration appears to spill over into the meeting itself. For example, we observed that when meetings started ten minutes late, besides creating frustration, members were more likely to interrupt one another throughout the meeting. Taken together, it is not surprising that meetings that started late resulted in lower-quality outcomes such as fewer new ideas and fewer good ideas.

Dropping five to ten minutes off the meeting length allows for transition time and helps mitigate future meeting lateness. While transition times are typical in school settings, Google may be responsible for starting this trend in corporate settings. At the very least, Google has given the practice a great deal of momentum. Larry Page, Google's cofounder and former CEO, returned to the company in April 2011. In one of his first memos to employees, he argued that hour-long meetings must allow for a bathroom break in between. This started the fifty/twenty-five rule I described earlier: one-hour meetings shortened to fifty minutes, and thirty-minute meetings shortened to twenty-five minutes. Since that time, this rule has been adopted by a host of companies across industries. One employee from PricewaterhouseCoopers (PwC) whom I interviewed told me that the company implemented a campaign initiative called "PwC has gone Google." "There was definitely more of an attitude of 'let's try to have a fifty-minute meeting,'" she said. The employee continued, "Also, I personally felt (and noticed others do this too) that I could legitimately excuse myself at the fifty-minute mark when I needed to travel to another meeting/prep for the other meeting, etc."

If you are interested in exploring this strategy, here is some good news: Google is making these speedier meetings easier than ever for non-Googlers to carry out. Now when you use the Google Calendar application, you can go into settings and actually change the default meeting length. There is a toggle switch for "speedy meetings" with a description reading, "encourage meeting efficiency and get to your next meeting on time." New meeting requests will then default to twenty-five- or fifty-minute increments. Although scheduling in this fashion will indeed speed up the meeting, I am also enthusiastic about a new concept bubbling up in more and more organizations—the super-speedy meeting.

The Super-Speedy Meeting

A ten- or fifteen-minute meeting is another tool for a leader to consider. These types of meetings are quite common in high-stakes workplaces like military, emergency (e.g., fire departments), and hospital settings. In these environments, short meetings are often used to debrief or actively reflect on an event or occurrence like an accident (e.g., what worked and what didn't work and why). The research on these types of meetings is enthusiastically supportive of their ability to enhance future individual and team performance and the safety behaviors of attendees. Short meetings with a focused agenda, facilitated effectively, can have tremendously positive effects. Plus, these short meetings align with research on limited human attention spans and fatigue.

Short meetings are spreading among companies quite rapidly. Percolate, a global technology firm, has set their default length for meetings at fifteen minutes. While they may adjust it up or down, they are committed to making fifteen minutes the typical meeting time. Similarly, Marissa Mayer, formerly a senior executive at Google and president/CEO of Yahoo, was famous for her short meetings. She would create large time blocks filled with ten-minute meeting windows. While this would often result in seventy meetings per week for her, this practice allowed her to be highly responsive to employee needs, it made getting a meeting on her calendar much easier, and it helped projects and initiatives to keep pushing forward without delays. She also claimed that by limiting the meetings to ten minutes, employees came in with a tight and highly focused agenda that promoted success. Highly focused and short are also the hallmarks of a final type of short meeting I want to profile: the huddle.

In sports, a huddle is a common activity that may be planned or spontaneous and that occurs before or after an action. At RSC Bio Solutions, a company whose practices we looked at in Chapter 3, the huddle is a gathering of the team to strategize, discuss, monitor, motivate, or celebrate. The concept of the huddle is being applied more than ever in a range of organizations, from Apple, to Dell, to Zappos, to Ritz Carlton, to Capital One. It was also used in the Obama White House. Logistically, a huddle in the business realm typically:

- Is ten or fifteen minutes in length
- Occurs at the same time each day (or every other day)
- Starts and ends on time
- Is done in the morning

- Occurs in the same place
- Involves the same people
- Mandates perfect attendance: if folks can't attend in person, they attend remotely
- Occurs standing up, if possible

Although each leader (or other attendees if serving in the role of facilitator) can customize a huddle according to the needs of the organization and team, it is often the case that one question from one or more of the following categories is used:

What Has Happened and Any Key Wins	What Will Happen
• What did you accomplish since yesterday? • What did you finish since yesterday? • Any key wins for you or the team that you can share? • Any key client updates?	• What are you working on today? • What is your top priority for the day? • What is the one most important thing you will get done today? • What are your top three priorities for the day or the week?
Key Metrics	Obstacles
• How are we doing on our company's top three metrics? • How are we doing on your team's top three metrics?	• What obstacles are impeding your progress? • Any "stuck points" you are facing? • Any roadblocks the team can help with? • Anything slowing down your progress?

You can also tailor your questions on the basis of emergent priorities and needs. For example, a company I worked with was trying to promote more cross-departmental teamwork. Thus, each week, one huddle was designed to explicitly align with that goal. This took a few different forms. For example, attendees might discuss roadblocks, such as work processes that may be hurting teamwork. Or, they may focus on the positive and ask attendees for examples of how others helped them and displayed teamwork. Or, they may ask each attendee to specify an emergent need he or she needs help with. Taken together, the organization was able to reinforce the current initiative and even monitor progress.

When you implement the huddle, all attendees should quickly answer all questions posed by the facilitator, unless of course there are extenuating circumstances. The meeting leader should make it clear that employees' answers should be succinct, to promote efficiency. It is also important for the meeting leader to stress that the huddle is not about reporting to the leader (this can be emphasized by rotating facilitator responsibilities). Instead, the huddle is about the team members communicating with one another, pulling together, learning together, and seeking ways to support each other. Relatedly, given the tight time limits of huddles, it is important to recognize that huddles are often about setting the table for additional conversations between team members offline. While quick suggestions and guidance can be shared during the huddle from attendee to attendee, if the issue involves a small subset of attendees, they can continue the conversation after the huddle is done. In fact, the walk to and from the huddle often turns out to be a rich opportunity for communication. Or, if the issue is substantive and involves most of the attendees, this issue can be taken up in a separate meeting.

Inc. magazine did a nice feature in 2007 called "The Art of the Huddle," highlighting how various leaders are leveraging their huddles. Let me share a couple of examples they profiled.

Bishop-Wisecarver, a $20 million maker of machine components

Huddles were initiated to improve communication across silos and departments (people were not talking enough to one another). The CEO reports that teamwork improved greatly once information sharing in huddles became routine. She indicates that snafus have been averted, with different managers making adjustments and offering support as they learned about issues and challenges in other departments.

Advanced Facilities Services, a $10 million
facilities management company

The CEO initiated huddles with his top managers to keep all of them focused on strategic long-term issues. Each manger takes less than a minute to indicate what he or she will do to advance the quarterly and yearly goals, progress made the previous day, and roadblocks being encountered. These conversations keep the team moving forward and allow the CEO to see if someone is off course or if any misunderstandings are occurring.

Overall, huddles promote a sense of unity, facilitate coordination, get needed information out there quickly, enable problem-solving, promote accountability, reveal blind spots, sharpen collective focus, foster action, promote better communication, enhance understanding of goals, and stimulate attendees to help one another achieve success.

Short Meetings Come with a Few Warnings

One worry often associated with the daily huddle is that people are just too busy to engage in this practice (e.g., they find it hard to find time on a daily basis for something like this). I can certainly see where this is coming from: if you are swamped with work, finding time to meet frequently is a genuine challenge. From my experience implementing huddles at organizations and examining data on their effectiveness, however, they are actually small-time investments yielding big returns. By improving coordination and communication among the members of a team, time is ultimately saved in the form of less rework, more teamwork, more support, and fewer miscommunications that need to be resolved. That being said, there are two important hazards to actively guard against when engaging in these practices.

The first hazard is creating yet more time spent in meetings. Shorter meetings are designed to replace some longer meetings. In other words, the hope is that some current longer meetings can be dropped as a result of these frequent and effective huddles. Keeping that in mind, it is certainly acceptable and appropriate to schedule additional meetings in response to topics that emerge in huddles and topics that are not completely discussed. One organization I know instituted something called "magic time." Basically, this was a standing meeting hour that the team kept open, no matter what, every other week (e.g., every other Monday at 10 a.m.); if a critical issue emerged in a huddle that needed substantive discussion (e.g., a key manufacturing challenge), all team members knew that this time was available for follow-up. Thus, the huddle did not run over the scheduled end time, which brings us to the second hazard.

A second key hazard to avoid is not honoring the shorter meeting times. Running over the scheduled huddle end time is highly problematic. Our research suggests, in fact, that running late may have more negative consequences on attendees than starting late: it serves to negatively affect any scheduled activities post-meeting, and by ending late, the meeting is breaking an implicit time contract of sorts with attendees. Breaking this "contract" results in stress, dissatisfaction, and frustration among attendees, which not only affects them personally but also can spill over to how they interact with others. By honoring the end time, you work to mitigate these issues. Beyond this benefit, the increased sense of urgency from a short meeting, with a hard stop time, will decrease rambling and unproductive, off-topic conversation.

A number of organizations take the practice of ending on time very seriously. Google often features a giant timer on the wall. The timer counts down the time remaining for a particular meeting or topic and is visible so that all know it and see it. O3 World, a design and product development agency, leverages technology they created, called Roombot, to keep meetings from ending late. This technology will warn attendees as the meeting's end time approaches and will even start dimming the lights. Of course, there are effective interventions to keep meetings on track that are not so technologically advanced.

Many companies tend to take a more humorous approach to getting meetings to end on time. At Tripping.com, the meeting leader must contribute to the team beer jar if the meeting does not end on time. Or, even more extreme, at Buddytruk, if the meeting runs over, the last person talking has to do fifty push-ups. It is clear that these companies recognize the benefits of ending on time, and recognize the importance of gaining buy-in from the attendees.

To help you get started conducting huddles, a Huddle Implementation Checklist tool is provided at the end of the book.

The Final Argument for Adding Short Meetings to Your Toolbox

As we have seen, there are so many reasons to leverage shorter meetings. If you're still not convinced, then try short meetings for your health. This is a bit of a leap, but there is a kernel of truth here. Research on physical meeting spaces was conducted by the Lawrence Berkeley National Laboratory on behalf of the US Department of Energy. To no surprise, as people exhale, carbon dioxide readings in confined spaces like meeting rooms increase. Researchers found that exposure to carbon dioxide for extended periods of time actually resulted in a decrease of constructive meeting processes like taking initiative and thinking strategically. Granted, they found that these negative effects did not kick in until after two and a half hours, but if you're looking for a physiological rationale for shorter meetings, it's there.

Let me close this section with a final piece of advice right out of the Steve Jobs playbook, one that I firmly believe in. The meeting leader should never be afraid, no matter the length of a meeting, to end a meeting early: (1) when it looks as if the meeting goals have been met (no need to drag it out), or (2) when the attendees seem to be just spinning their wheels and are not being productive. In the case of the latter, sometimes just stopping and regrouping at a later time or using a different communication medium (e.g., email) can be just what is needed to ultimately turn a losing effort into a winning one.

Takeaways

1. Parkinson's law states that work expands to whatever time is allotted. Keep this in mind with regard to meetings, and take the time to conscientiously choose the length of your meetings (based on the goals, agenda, attendees, etc.). Perhaps even consider a nontraditional meeting length or start time, like the forty-eight-minute meeting, to push the envelope.
2. Consider shortening your regular meetings by five to ten minutes (instead of thirty or sixty minutes, try twenty-five or fifty). Not only will this create a little added pressure, which is shown to make attendees more effective, but also it will reduce lateness to meetings and allow for breaks between meetings.
3. Consider the idea of implementing daily or weekly short meetings or huddles. These ten- to fifteen-minute meetings should have a focused agenda, involve lots of concise interaction among attendees, and be facilitated effectively using some of the key questions I have included in this chapter.
4. Although short meetings or huddles can be very effective, it is important to keep two things in mind: (1) certain emergent topics may need their own dedicated meeting time outside the huddle context, and (2) always start and end these quick meetings on time to maximize their effectiveness and attendees' satisfaction.

Chapter 5
AGENDAS ARE
A HOLLOW CRUTCH

Throughout history, you can find examples of a traveling "merchant" coming into town selling ointments, pills, elixirs, and objects promising quick fixes to problems concerning health, love, wealth, enemies, or even bad bosses. Sales were good for these merchants. Customers are reliably drawn to quick fixes to complicated problems. After all, quick fixes do not require deep thought, careful analysis, or nuance, nor do they require hard work. The other hallmark of a quick fix is the rarity of it actually working. The volumes of books and articles that claim they will help you improve your organization's meetings typically have one key idea in common—they espouse the "must do" advice of having an agenda and claim this as a cure-all. Unfortunately, relying on a meeting agenda is a quick fix, and not one that on its own will make a difference.

It is hard to find a business book on meetings that does not start with the importance of creating a meeting agenda. However, the research on agendas is far from enthusiastic. Two studies I published early in my career examined the best ways to design meetings. In both studies, a leader's decision to have an agenda was a very minor predictor of attendees' perceptions of meeting effectiveness. More pessimistically, other researchers found no positive relationship between attendees' evaluation of meeting quality and having a written agenda. Taken together, the conclusion is that agendas in and of themselves do little to improve meetings. Furthermore, it is often the case that agendas are recycled from meeting to meeting. In 2003, Marakon Associates and *The Economist* Intelligence Unit studied top management teams across 197 companies worldwide. These were large companies with sales of at least $500 million. They reported that in half of the companies they studied, the agendas from top management teams were either exactly the same from meeting to meeting or they were created in an ad hoc, spontaneous fashion. In reflecting on my own client work, I have seen so many instances where the only thing changing agenda-wise from meeting to meeting in a department was the date in the upper left corner.

In the rest of this chapter I will discuss ways to avoid the generic-agenda pitfall. I will cover the process of constructing an agenda from a number of strategic vantage points, including implementing a goals and decisions focus, how to order items, how to engage others in the process, the notion of directly responsible individuals, and other key topics in agenda creation. Ultimately, this chapter is about moving beyond just having an agenda and instead creating an agenda that truly can be transformative—an agenda heeding the sage advice of Ben Franklin, "by failing to prepare, you are preparing to fail."

Planning a ~~Wedding~~ Meeting

An agenda is an event plan. When planning an event, we think carefully about the details, the flow, the experience, and the approach. The same mindset and process should occur when planning a meeting. In fact, the notion of thinking of a meeting as an event is really not a stretch. It is not unusual for a meeting to cost between $1,000 and $3,000 in attendee time and salaries, which many would likely say is a fairly expensive event warranting careful planning. Related to this, as a meeting leader, you are in the unique position of being a steward of others' time and experience. We would never go to a client meeting unprepared, nor would we conduct a workshop for others without planning; the same focus should be brought to a meeting. Prepare for an internal meeting like you would prepare a client event, even for just a few minutes. This starts with thinking through what truly needs to be accomplished for the meeting to be successful.

Meetings should be called to address issues that require genuine interaction among and engagement with attendees. While meetings can certainly have an "update" component, which is only natural, this should be a small part of the meeting, relatively speaking. If the topic does not require interaction, another communication medium would likely be more efficient (e.g., a memo, webinar).

Agenda Construction: What Should Be Included in the Meeting?

The following are some examples of topics particularly well suited for a meeting; these are the types of interaction-requiring topics you would like to see on an agenda:

- Identification of key risks or challenges the unit is facing or will be facing
- Identification and discussion of key metrics to assess progress
- Evaluation of key processes or changes made
- Discussion of what is going well and not so well—areas of improvement
- Dissemination and interpretation of key information or policy changes
- Calls to action and planning or strategy activities
- Solving important problems and making collective decisions
- After action, reflection and discussion of key learnings
- Discussion and celebration of victories and individual and collective excellence
- Short-range and long-range forecasting

- Identification and discussion of new opportunities
- Dialogue around coordination of efforts
- Budgetary planning, issues, and adjustments
- Key talent issues, both positive and negative
- Presenting a new product or idea and getting feedback

In addition to this list, ideas for the agenda should also bubble up from the attendees or team members themselves. After all, a meeting is a shared experience, and it seems only appropriate to allow all parties to have some level of input. Andy Grove, the former CEO of Intel, whom I mentioned in Chapter 3, once said, "The most important criterion governing matters to be talked about is that they be issues that preoccupy and nag the subordinate." Research strongly supports the notion of "voice" in work-related activities. That is, when employees are encouraged to share their thoughts and ideas in a genuine manner and those ideas are truly heard, they tend to feel a greater sense of commitment to and identification with the team and the organization. This translates into a meeting setting in the form of an engaged attendee, one who is fully plugged into the meeting itself. By adding employee input to the meeting agenda, you are increasing the chances of hitting topics of critical importance to all who are present. This all can be executed simply by sending an email three to five days before the meeting asking for topics to include on the agenda (I sometimes recommend having attendees include a reason why this agenda item should be included). While asking for your team's input, it is important to keep in mind that you are ultimately in charge of the meeting. What employees propose should certainly be considered and taken seriously. However, if you deem the suggestion *not* to be a good agenda item for the upcoming meeting, you should either (1) address the issue with the employee or subset of employees outside the meeting or (2) move it to a future meeting. The only thing you should not do is pretend you never received the suggestion; some form of closing the loop is needed.

After identifying the *potential* topics and goals of the meeting (emerging both from self-reflection and from others' input), as the meeting leader you need to carefully reflect on the importance of the goals and whether each is adding true value—value beyond opportunity costs (i.e., time that could be spent elsewhere). Drop content that does not make the cut. Also, drop content if the goal is only relevant to a small subset of attendees; in this case, it is best pursued in a different context.

Agenda Construction: Flow Matters

The next step in agenda creation involves the critical task of *ordering the topics,* which is essential to the success of the meeting. A nice study on agenda order was conducted by psychology professors Glen Littlepage and Julie Poole from Middle Tennessee State University in the early 1990s. These professors conducted an experiment involving twenty-four meetings, each with three to five attendees. Each meeting group was given an agenda and asked to conduct its meeting. The researchers were able to track time spent on various agenda items, with each agenda item differing in difficulty and importance. Most interestingly, they also manipulated the order of agenda items. Agendas included items such as the selection of a temporary secretary and the purchase of six hundred computers for the organization. To highlight a few key findings, the researchers found that weighty items did not always garner more time; most importantly, the items early in the agenda received a disproportionate amount of time and attention. The bottom line: order clearly matters. Adopting a strategy where agenda items are simply listed in the order received (e.g., first in, first on), or without critical thought, is highly counterproductive.

Given these findings, first and foremost, I recommend ranking your prospective meeting goals (both those from you and those from your employees) on the basis of strategic importance. You need to have a good sense of what you feel is essential to cover, versus what is just nice to cover. With that said, issues affecting the here and now should not be automatically privileged over issues that have a longer time horizon. It is critical that meetings not be fully focused on putting out fires and solving immediate problems but instead also contain some more proactive, longer-term items.

Now that you have this information at hand, you can start making decisions leveraging the following rules of thumb. First, it might be the case in looking at your agenda items that certain items should be addressed in close proximity to one another. By doing so, your agenda will tell a better "story." Second, if all else is generally equal, I like the idea of prioritizing employee-generated agenda items. This sends a strong message around voice, inclusion, and shared ownership. Third, although meetings should always start on time and all items on the agenda should be important, the very first part of the meeting can contain some "warm-up" types of items, thus serving as a little buffer if individuals are late and, more importantly, as a means to build momentum (e.g., sharing quick announcements, sharing quick updates from the last meeting). However, no later than 10–15 percent into the meeting time should the most important, meaty, and critical agenda items be broached. This not only ensures coverage of these topics but also gets attendees hooked early and engaged in the meeting. I agree with author Patrick Lencioni, who wrote in his book *Death by Meetings*, "Leaders of meetings need to do the same by putting the right issues— often the most controversial ones—on the table at the beginning of their meetings. By demanding that their people wrestle with those issues until resolution has been achieved, they can create genuine, compelling drama, and prevent their audiences from checking out."

The points just made will help greatly in crafting your agenda "story." It is also important to note that no matter what story agenda path you take, it should always end in a similar way—closing with a few-minutes-long wrap-up to cover meeting takeaways, clarify assignments, and note some items that will be put on the agenda for next time. I also recommend that you sometimes end the meeting with a Q&A session. This is basically just an "open swim" to promote good communication in the team. These sessions can include questions that employees have about topics covered in the meeting or topics not covered in the meeting. To avoid having an awkward silence, some leaders establish the number of questions to be asked, thus ensuring that the time is used (e.g., "before we end the meeting I would like to answer five questions that folks have").

This text lays out the key steps and decision points in building a quality agenda. However, as I mentioned earlier in this chapter, an agenda alone is not a cure-all. We've all sat through meetings where carefully built agendas were ignored. The next step involves the use of the agenda in the meeting. Before you go live with your agenda, there are two things you must consider: the first is whether you want to assign times to agenda items, and the second pertains to whether you want to assign discussion or responsibility leaders for agenda items. Let me discuss each of these next.

To Time or Not to Time?

Should time allotments be assigned to agenda items? It's complicated. First, we know from goal-setting research that time allocated to agenda items should serve to drive action, provide a sense of focus, and promote completion. However, research generally indicates that too much structure can serve to derail creativity, enjoyment, and flexibility. Furthermore, recall from our discussion of Parkinson's law that we tend to unconsciously and consciously match our efforts to allocated time. Thus, discussion will be influenced by the allotment. This could be positive or negative depending on whether the time allocated does justice to the agenda item in question. The primary concern is that if there *is* a mismatch, the quality of the discussion around the agenda item will be sacrificed.

One response to this concern is an obvious one: the meeting leader can alter allotments in real time, based on the discussion at hand. Although this sounds like a simple fix, we've already noted how seldom "quick fixes" are true solutions. Real-time adjustments are, in reality, a tricky solution to execute, as (1) in the moment, it can be hard to recognize the need for an adjustment, especially as we are biased by our own perspective; and (2) doing this creates a precedent and potentially a norm of not honoring future timed agenda items—in essence, defeating the purpose of setting time allotments. Taken together, the decision to use a timed agenda is indeed complicated.

Following are my personal rules of thumb for determining whether a leader should use timed agenda items. Note that my preference is to think of a timed agenda as a tool one can leverage occasionally, some of the time, all of the time, or never. If you answer "yes" to one or more of the following questions, a timed agenda is worth considering.

- Do attendees tend to get caught up and dwell on minutia?
- Do attendees tend to veer off course and into tangents?
- Are you noticing that your meetings are highly routine and do you think trying something new might spice things up (this assumes that timed agendas are not something currently in place)?
- Have you used timed agendas in the past with these attendees and did it work well?
- Are you hoping to integrate guest attendees at one or more points in the meeting where they are needed but don't want to hold them captive for the entire meeting? Timed agendas are an effective and efficient way to do

this. For example, certain individuals can arrive and leave at set times corresponding to the agenda timing. I will flesh this out more in Chapter 6 when discussing the management of meeting size.

- Are there certain topics on the agenda that you want to be sure get the deep attention they need?

If you decide to take the timed agenda path, think carefully about what time to assign to each item—clearly time should be allocated by item importance. That said, anticipating time needs for an agenda item is still tricky, as it is hard to anticipate questions, different points of view, and conflict. I always encourage leaders to share draft item times with another meeting attendee before finalizing the agenda; the extra feedback is helpful in getting it right. Finally, if you do proceed with timed items, don't forget to gather feedback periodically to assess whether the overall use of the technique is working and whether your time allotments have been appropriate.

Sharing Meeting Responsibilities and Assigning Agenda Item Owners

Although meeting leaders are ultimately in charge of the meeting experience, they have the ability to share leadership in a strategic manner. One way of doing this is to have certain agenda items assigned to "owners." These owners facilitate the discussion around the agenda item and, in many cases, are in charge of the post-meeting actions related to it. The research literature shows that when you clearly and publicly attach a name to a task, you foster accountability. This, in turn, increases follow-through on what was decided at the meeting (an important piece of ultimate meeting success). This type of practice is embraced by a number of organizations. Perhaps most notably, it has become a standard meeting practice for Apple. Apple initiated the concept of a

"DRI"—a directly responsible individual. A DRI is assigned to agenda items for all to see. Employees expect to see a DRI next to an agenda item, and everyone knows that the DRI will be driving action. In addition to this utilitarian purpose, a DRI serves a number of other purposes, including (1) getting more people involved in the meeting, (2) providing a nice opportunity for skill development in leading meetings, and (3) making the meeting more stimulating for other attendees as more voices are incorporated. Note that it may be the case that the DRI is identified not prior to discussion of the agenda but at the meeting itself, post-discussion. Regardless, the key is to have a DRI.

Matching a Process with Agenda Item

The final step in agenda creation that is so commonly ignored is thinking about processes to use to address the various agenda items in play. Stated differently, planning a meeting is knowing not only *what* you want to cover but also *how you want to go about doing it*. This book, especially Chapter 9, is chock-full of various tools and techniques to consider when addressing various agenda items. Look for opportunities to leverage them in a manner that is helpful. Consider the people, the tasks, the history, and the potential pitfalls when picking the right tool for the job. Meeting leaders are uniquely positioned to do this activity, given their big-picture focus and their key role in ensuring there is a great return on the meeting-time investment.

Putting the Pieces Together

Although meeting agendas come in many different forms and one size does not fit all, in the outline that follows I put this chapter's suggestions together and share an example of an excellent meeting agenda:

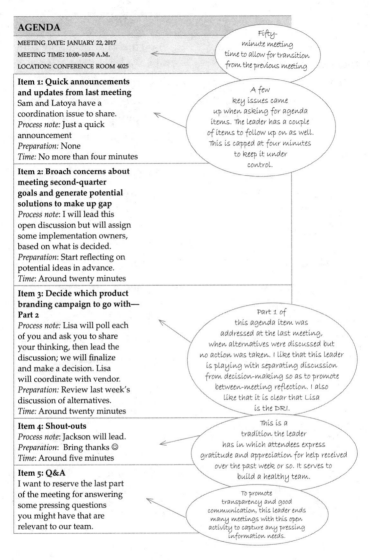

AGENDA

MEETING DATE: JANUARY 22, 2017

MEETING TIME: 10:00–10:50 A.M.

LOCATION: CONFERENCE ROOM 4025

Fifty-minute meeting time to allow for transition from the previous meeting

Item 1: Quick announcements and updates from last meeting
Sam and Latoya have a coordination issue to share.
Process note: Just a quick announcement
Preparation: None
Time: No more than four minutes

A few key issues came up when asking for agenda items. The leader has a couple of items to follow up on as well. This is capped at four minutes to keep it under control.

Item 2: Broach concerns about meeting second-quarter goals and generate potential solutions to make up gap
Process note: I will lead this open discussion but will assign some implementation owners, based on what is decided.
Preparation: Start reflecting on potential ideas in advance.
Time: Around twenty minutes

Item 3: Decide which product branding campaign to go with—Part 2
Process note: Lisa will poll each of you and ask you to share your thinking, then lead the discussion; we will finalize and make a decision. Lisa will coordinate with vendor.
Preparation: Review last week's discussion of alternatives.
Time: Around twenty minutes

Part 1 of this agenda item was addressed at the last meeting, when alternatives were discussed but no action was taken. I like that this leader is playing with separating discussion from decision-making so as to promote between-meeting reflection. I also like that it is clear that Lisa is the DRI.

Item 4: Shout-outs
Process note: Jackson will lead.
Preparation: Bring thanks ☺
Time: Around five minutes

This is a tradition the leader has in which attendees express gratitude and appreciation for help received over the past week or so. It serves to build a healthy team.

Item 5: Q&A
I want to reserve the last part of the meeting for answering some pressing questions you might have that are relevant to our team.

To promote transparency and good communication, this leader ends many meetings with this open activity to capture any pressing information needs.

To help you with your agenda efforts, an Agenda Template tool is provided at the end of the book.

Finally, let me close this chapter with some questions I commonly get about agendas that we have not yet covered.

How far in advance should an agenda be distributed?

Generally, two to three days is a fine rule of thumb. Sending the agenda in advance is especially helpful if the agenda requires some preparation from the attendees. Noting what preparation is needed will help to promote a focused meeting. In Chapter 9, we will look at a meeting practice where the first part of the meeting is actually dedicated to preparation: in other words, instead of asking people to prepare in advance, time is allocated at the start of the meeting to do the preparatory work. This ensures, of course, that everyone begins the discussion with the same amount of preparation. More on this later.

How rigid should you be on following the agenda?

There are times when you, as meeting leader, may have to be spontaneous and reorganize the agenda given some emergent crisis or event that occurred just prior to the meeting. Although this is certainly less than optimal, sometimes there is no other choice. It is okay to demonstrate thoughtful flexibility.

What is something you have seen a leader do as part of the agenda that was surprising and well received?

While you don't want to overuse this technique because it may not come across as sincere, one leader shares at the end of meetings some fairly specific feedback around something each attendee did during the meeting that she felt was particularly helpful in creating a better experience for all. This positive reinforcement can increase the likelihood that the mentioned behaviors will continue to occur.

Can you cancel a meeting if you just don't have compelling agenda topics?

Yes, yes, please yes, yes, certainly, a must, and yes.

Takeaways

1. Almost all business books on improving workplace meetings tout the meeting agenda as an instrumental tool. However, research shows that simply having a meeting agenda does not, in and of itself, result in a more satisfying or effective meeting.

2. In order for agendas to be effective, meeting leaders have to be intentional about their creation—agenda planning needs to be thought out carefully and approached with care, much like the process of planning an event. A good tip for making an agenda that is tailored to the needs of the team or organization—and will also increase accountability—is to reach out to attendees for agenda items.

3. In terms of other ideas for increasing the effectiveness of an agenda, I advise that meeting leaders place items that have to be covered near the top of the agenda. I also believe that the decision to use time allotments should be made on a meeting-by-meeting basis—they are not necessary for effectiveness, but they have their place. Finally, it is a good option to assign "owners" to agenda items in order to increase accountability.

4. Remember: keep your agendas fresh! Refrain from using the same agenda with only a new date. If you do not normally have time allotments, try including them. If you always have status updates at the beginning of the meeting, consider moving them toward the end. If you have employees who never participate, consider assigning them an agenda item to own. Agendas and meetings should not become stale.

Chapter 6
THE BIGGER, THE BADDER

In preparation for this chapter, I interviewed employee "Joe S. Lacker." Joe was a big fan of large meetings. Although Joe is a fictional character, he is saying things that came directly out of interviews I have conducted.

> ME: *Thank you for chatting with me, Joe. Is it true that you love huge meetings?*
>
> JOE: *Oh yes, the bigger the better. My ideal situation is a big meeting where there are actually not enough chairs around the table and I have to sit against the back wall away from the action.*
>
> ME: *Tell me more about your joy of big meetings.*
>
> JOE: *They are just so relaxing.*
>
> ME: *Wow, I was not expecting that. Can you elaborate?*
>
> JOE: *Large meetings are just a nice opportunity for me to recline, enjoy the clever contributions of a couple of my colleagues who are just so funny in big groups, and catch up on some emails.*
>
> ME: *Hmmm.*
>
> JOE: *Along with some well-timed head nods, I do set a goal of contributing once or twice just so folks remember that I was there. Although most of these large meetings are really not all that relevant to my job, the added bonus is that I do tend to learn one new thing over the course of the hour.*

Big meetings, otherwise known as "bloated" meetings, are a fixture of organizational life. When I have done organizational meeting "audits" for clients, a common finding is employee concern about meetings having too many attendees, with over 50 percent of meetings containing two or more unnecessary attendees, given the stated meeting goals. Typically, this occurs out of a spirit of inclusiveness, an attitude of "the more the merrier," an unwillingness to actually analyze who is truly needed given the meeting goals, and fear of political repercussions associated with excluding someone. Regardless of the motives, large meetings are undoubtedly suboptimal from a process and effectiveness perspective. In addition to sharing the evidence around the problems of large meetings, in this chapter, I discuss managing and shrinking meeting size without engendering a sense of exclusion in non-attendees.

The Case against Big Meetings: A Review of the Evidence

The horsepower of any meeting comes from the knowledge, skills, and abilities of the meeting attendees themselves. Thus it follows that as meeting size increases, more resources and perspectives can be brought to bear on the goals of the meeting— namely, more voices, more ideas, more information, and more brains to catch errors. In theory, this *should* lead to enhanced meeting effectiveness. Unfortunately, this does not appear to be the case. Marcia Blenko, Michael Mankins, and Paul Rogers, authors of *Decide & Deliver: 5 Steps to Breakthrough Performance in Your Organization*, discuss research conducted with data from Bain & Company. They report that for each additional person over seven members in a decision-making group, decision effectiveness is *reduced* by approximately 10 percent. Certainly, this math does not bode well for large meetings! Another study recently published in *Group Dynamics: Theory Research and Practice* examined the relationship between the size of a team and the quality of the group experience. In a survey of ninety-seven work teams, larger teams reported poorer-quality group experiences and higher levels of counterproductive behaviors, including more interpersonal aggression, more self-centered behaviors, and greater misuse of resources.

It is clear that larger meetings bring with them increased coordination challenges; the additional voices and viewpoints over and above the "essential personnel" can become unwieldy to manage and integrate. Perhaps even more noteworthy, we know that as meeting size increases, the probability of the "social disease" called *social loafing* increases. Social loafing is a human tendency to reduce effort and motivation when working in a collective; it is akin to "hiding in a crowd," as Joe S. Lacker illustrated in his interview starting this chapter. Max Ringelmann, a French professor of agricultural engineering, discovered this phenomenon in an incredibly novel way: an experiment involving tug of war. Volunteers were told to pull on a rope as hard as they could, but they did so in groups of different sizes. The rope was attached to a device to measure force/strain so that the researchers knew how much they pulled as individuals and as part of collectives. Results showed that as group size increased, collective performance was incrementally lower than would be expected from simple addition of individual performances. Individuals in dyads performed to 93 percent of their ability, individuals in triads pulled to 85 percent of ability, and individuals in groups of eight pulled to 49 percent of their ability on average. These findings have been replicated in a host of different contexts. A recent study even looked at screaming: dyads shouted at 66 percent of what they did individually, and groups of six shouted at 36 percent of what they did as individuals. Taken together, it is clear that we pull less when we know others are around to pull. We don't give it our all; we shirk.

As meeting size increases, process inefficiencies and process problems increase given coordination issues and the like. Thus, the larger the meeting, the less optimally the meeting group performs, on average. The ultimate challenge, therefore, is to have the right number of attendees—not too few, and not too many. Not only is this good for meeting quality, it is also ultimately good for the employee; our past research shows that when individuals attend meetings not relevant to their job, their employee engagement erodes. I'll now tee up the all-important questions: how do you decide who should attend the meeting, and what is the magic number?

It Starts with the Goals of the Meeting

In the next sections, I present a series of suggestions and techniques that should help you decide whom to invite to your meetings. To start with the obvious, the meeting leader should consider the goals of the meeting. For each meeting goal, the leader should ponder the following questions:

1. Who has the *information and knowledge* about the topic in question?
2. Who are the key decision makers and important stakeholders relevant to the issue?
3. Who are the people who *need the information* that is going to be discussed?
4. Who are the people who will *implement* any decision or act on the issue?

These questions can help you identify the relevant and necessary parties but still may result in a meeting with too many attendees.

Meeting Size: Rules of Thumb

Some companies try to create implicit norms to manage meeting size more broadly. Percolate, a technology company, created six meeting rules they distribute widely to employees, including by posting them on their website. One of the rules is "no spectators." Apple works to stay true to Steve Jobs's intolerance of large meetings. Two stories in particular have become Apple lore, continuing to shape Apple culture. First, Steve Jobs was known to (politely) throw people out of his meetings when he thought they just were not needed there. Second, and most famously, when President Obama called tech leaders to Washington, DC, for a meeting, Jobs refused to attend—just too many people there for it to be an effective use of time.

Aside from building cultural resistance to large meetings through communications and stories, there are some general rules of thumb that companies often propagate to their employees. Google often advocates no more than ten people being in any one meeting. Amazon has used what they call the "two-pizza rule": the meeting should not contain more people than what two pizzas could feed. One manufacturing firm was so committed to keeping meetings small that they created a policy that meetings could not include more than seven people unless approved by a more senior manager.

Some rules of thumb can also be found in the meetings literature. For example, there is the 8-18-1800 rule. This guideline basically suggests that if you are trying to solve a problem or make a decision, keep the meeting to eight people or less. Brainstorming, however, could include up to eighteen people. Then, if the meeting is to just inform the troops and rally folks together, you can have eighteen hundred or more. In addition, John Kello, independent consultant extraordinaire who also studies meetings, advocates a rule of seven given the extensive social psychological research on small groups and effectiveness. This is consistent with my guidelines as well. Seven or fewer is the ideal group size for decision-making and problem-solving. Eight to twelve attendees is doable if the leader has outstanding facilitation skills. For idea generation, agenda setting, and huddles, fewer than fifteen individuals is ideal. Overall, a meeting leader wants to have the leanest meeting possible given the goals at hand.

Smaller Meetings and Hurt Feelings

Grousing about meetings is a foundational activity of most workplaces. We tend to complain readily about too many meetings. The one thing worse than having too many meetings, however, is the feeling of being excluded from meetings. Not receiving a meeting invite when we believe the content touches us even superficially creates worries about marginalization, isolation, and impotence. As much as it pains us to admit, being invited to a meeting is often viewed as an indicator of organizational self-worth and promotes feelings of being valued.

While we might complain loudly about invitations to so many meetings, in truth, on some level, we relish the invitations.

Most meeting leaders want to avoid having others feel excluded, especially as they try to uphold organizational values reflecting high levels of collaboration, voice, and inclusion. By inviting lots of people to meetings, they feel as if they are enacting these values at a local level. Furthermore, they recognize the politics around meeting invitations—inviting certain people is just politically the right thing to do from a strategic vantage point. Taken together, as meeting leaders we are faced with a horrible quandary. Large meetings are not optimal, often leading to dysfunction and attendee dissatisfaction. Concurrently, excluding even tangentially relevant individuals can lead to hard feelings, angst, and burnt bridges. The challenge, then, is how can we avoid having spectators at meetings without engendering ill feelings? There are ways!

Techniques for Reducing Spectators That Don't Undermine Feelings of Inclusion

To reiterate, the ultimate goal is to only include those necessary to a meeting, but not to create feelings of exclusion among those not attending. There are five techniques to do this. First and foremost, in examining your agenda and the goals listed, it might be the case that you could split the agenda items in a compelling manner, thus allowing you to hold two smaller and shorter meetings rather than one larger, more expansive meeting. This allows you to keep meeting sizes in check.

The second technique leverages a timed-agenda approach described in the last chapter. With this technique, the meeting boundary becomes porous—certain individuals arrive at certain times and leave at certain times. This is an ideal approach for being highly inclusive but without feeling the weight of too many attendees. That being said, this can get a little messy at times with folks coming and going. But I don't see this as a bad thing per se. It helps to break rhythms and create energy.

The key issue, however, is to press upon those entering at particular times the need to be prompt. My preference is to have them arrive a few minutes before their assigned entry time to be sure everything runs smoothly. A spin-off of this approach, which I prefer, is to order the agenda items such that the first items are relevant to the larger group of folks, but then after that item is completed, a group of attendees leaves and the remaining individuals continue on with the meeting. In both cases, the agenda timing strategy allows one to tailor attendance to agenda items in a compelling and strategic manner.

Research has demonstrated that asking for input from others, even if none is subsequently provided, engenders feelings of support, buy-in, and an overall feeling of inclusion. These insights inform the approaches that follow. The third technique involves gathering input from ancillary individuals before the meeting, in lieu of requiring attendance. Let's say there are some individuals whose expertise may be of some relevance to a particular meeting, but, in general, it is really not all that consequential. If you want them to still feel some sense of voice, you can formally or informally survey these individuals in advance—they can provide input on a series of prompts that will be discussed in the meeting itself. This could include their ideas about topics, reactions to a topic, or other ideas for topics that should be discussed in the larger meeting. Please note, a response should not be required—but the key is that the opportunity is provided. At the meeting, when the agenda item arises, the meeting leader introduces the pre-meeting feedback received from the non-attendees. These reactions should be summarized and provided to attendees, perhaps as fodder to start the discussion. It need not alter discussion per se, but at least the content is made known in some capacity. Consequently, the non-attendee can feel some sense of connection to the meeting. Let me share a sample email as an example. Of course, the prompt will vary according to the meeting goals:

Dear Joel, Jane, Sandy, Sasha, and Gordon:

As you may have heard, there is a group of us meeting (Jacob, Jessica, Debbie, Noa, Pete, and Ivan) to talk about ideas on how to improve our vendor procurement process. We know that you have some experience with this process. We welcome any input you may have on the following questions:

1. *Ideas you have to improve the process?*
2. *Any key issues you think we should be aware of as we attempt to make improvements?*

If you could share your thoughts by end of day June 1, that would be ideal. I know you are very busy so you may not have time to respond to this email, but any input is certainly welcome. Thank you in advance. I am also happy to loop back after the meeting on what was discussed.

The fourth technique takes another page out of the Google playbook and is an ideal complement to technique #3. Bloomberg News did a profile of meetings at Google and reported that Google is committed to capturing a complete set of meeting notes. Further, meetings at Google often feature multiple displays. One display shows, for example, the presentation/materials (if applicable). Next to the presentation is the display of the meeting minutes being taken in real time so as to create focus and minimize inaccuracies. Detailed meeting notes are often taken (1) to help attendees remember what was actually said during the meeting, (2) to help attendees recognize that what they said was actually heard as it was documented, and, most importantly, (3) to promote post-meeting actions being taken by directly responsible individuals as recorded in the meeting. These notes, however, can also be used to promote feelings of inclusion among those *not attending* meetings. This is usually a forgotten purpose, as the typical practice is to distribute meeting notes only to attendees. What I want to advocate here is distributing the meeting notes to a host of secondary stakeholders who, while not involved in the meeting itself, are still affected by the issues discussed in the meeting. The meeting notes can be provided to them with an email that invites questions, comments, and other remarks that can inform the next meeting. Typically, no feedback is received, but the invitation to review the notes is deeply appreciated by the recipients and promotes positive feelings of inclusion. So, while inviting secondary stakeholders would likely have resulted in just spectators, this approach in concert with technique #3 becomes a happy medium. To help you with your note-taking efforts, the Guide to Taking Good Meeting Minutes and Notes is provided in the "Tools" section at the end of the book.

Let me close this technique with a piece of advice I shared at Siemens in a leadership development workshop I taught on meetings. I laid it out as a hypothetical conversation with a potential attendee who a meeting leader doesn't think is really essential to the meeting. At the same time, the meeting leader doesn't want to alienate the person:

> MEETING LEADER: *Jack, as you know, we are having a meeting to discuss initiative X. I am very sensitive about honoring your time. As I reflect on the agenda, I don't think your attendance is required per se. I also don't want you to feel left out. I would like to propose the following. I will make sure a very good set of notes is taken. I will then share the notes with you. If after reading the notes you think you would like to come to future meetings, we can definitely revisit this. Otherwise, I can just keep you in the loop. Seem reasonable? However, if you have any input on this topic, please just email me by Wednesday, and I will share it at the meeting.*

The outcome of this is almost unequivocally just appreciation and a continued desire to stay in the loop rather than attend. The bottom line is, by inviting input, by sharing meeting notes, and by keeping future invitations on the table, you mitigate others' feelings of isolation. Feelings of gratitude around having additional time, however, are amplified.

The fifth and final technique for decreasing meeting size is called "representative voices." In this approach the meeting leader asks certain individuals to explicitly represent a set of stakeholders; this becomes an additional meeting role the individual takes on. For example, one person, in addition to his or her own perspective, represents the voices of those in, say, Marketing and Sales. In this role, the representative is expected to connect with folks in that function before the meeting, keep them in the loop afterward, and ask for input as needed on an ongoing basis. This serves to keep meeting size down, but also supports feelings of inclusiveness. From my experience, when people are asked explicitly to take on a role like this and, importantly, it is communicated to all stakeholders, they usually do it in an engaged manner.

Some research indirectly speaks to this. Here is an example from outside the business context. A recent study published in the journal *Psychology, Crime & Law* examined how roles played out at a bus stop. Picture this: a confederate arrives and places a bag down before leaving to go to the ATM close by. The confederate either asks someone at the bus stop to watch his bag (direct commitment), asks everyone to just watch his bag (indirect commitment), or does not say anything and just goes to the ATM (control condition). Thirty seconds later, a different confederate walks up, picks up the bag, and quickly walks away in the opposite direction of the "victim." There were 150 participants observed. In the control condition (where no one was asked either directly or indirectly), someone intervened only 34 *percent* of the time. In the indirect commitment condition, someone intervened 56 percent of the time. In the direct commitment condition, however, someone intervened 88 *percent* of the time. Explicitly, being assigned a direct role resulted in more commitment to action.

Conclusion

Any time an unneeded employee is *not* at a meeting, you are giving the kindest gift one can give—the gift of time (both to the employee who doesn't have to attend the meeting and to the meeting attendees who are not wasting as much time tripping over unnecessary voices). Beyond this, you are taking steps to decrease frustration (again, of all parties), not to mention saving the company money by giving folks the ability to recoup lost time. But never forget the one thing people dislike more than meetings: not being invited to a meeting. Thus, by leveraging the techniques described in this chapter, not only will you manage meeting size more strategically, but also, most importantly, you will achieve this without risking isolation and exclusion of others.

Takeaways

1. Although it may seem that as meetings increase in size they would be more effective because of the greater number of ideas, resources, and brainpower, research shows that, unfortunately, this is not the case. To the contrary, having too many meeting attendees can actually reduce effectiveness because there can be too many voices, logistical challenges, and even social loafing.

2. While having too many attendees can be problematic, it is also important to realize that employees not receiving a meeting invitation can feel excluded. In fact, as we know from previous chapters, there is an innate need for humans to meet; thus, cutting down the invite list—in an effort to reduce confusion—can actually result in some unhappy employees.

3. In an attempt to advise on the "right" number of meeting attendees, I first recommend consulting your meeting goals to help you determine all the relevant and necessary parties. Thinking about who the key decision makers and stakeholders are for accomplishing each goal will help you make decisions about the invite list.

4. In addition to thinking through the goals of each meeting, consider a timed-agenda approach; this technique involves inviting different groups of employees to attend only a certain portion of a meeting that is most relevant to them. Another technique designed to make others not invited to the meeting feel included is to consult them before the meeting to get their input.

This helps them feel involved, without being in the meeting itself.

5. The final ideas I propose for keeping meetings to a manageable size (while preventing feelings of exclusion) are taking excellent notes and choosing "representative voices." Meeting notes should be taken in real time, distributed to all relevant parties following the meeting, and should include owners of action items. The other, the "voices" technique, involves assigning a meeting attendee to represent the collective interests of a group of stakeholders, such as a department, that is not invited to the meeting.

Chapter 7
DON'T GET TOO COMFORTABLE IN THAT CHAIR

Humans and habitual behaviors go hand in hand. Routines and rituals consciously and unconsciously fill our days, our months, our years. Duke University professors David Neal, Wendy Wood, and Jeffrey Quinn wrote a terrific review piece on the topic of habits in the journal *Current Directions in Psychological Science*. After reviewing the research literature, they found that roughly 45 percent of daily behaviors are repeated almost every day in the same location. Forty-five percent! Habitual behavior extends to collectives as well, be it in groups or even organizations.

Habits or routines aren't necessarily bad. Habits can be highly functional, enabling, and effective. The key, however, is that given our proclivity as individuals and as groups to be habitual, we may forget the importance of "mixing things up" and trying new things. In fact, we may not even be aware that we have become quite fixed in our approaches.

How does this apply to meetings? Leaders engage in a host of habitual meeting behaviors. For a moment, let's put aside the possibility that the meeting itself could, in fact, be occurring just out of habit. Beyond this, the meeting may be starting and ending at the same time, on the same day, with attendees sitting in the places they always sit in, in the same meeting room, and following the same basic agenda they always follow—all just another product of habit. In this chapter, I will discuss minor interventions to break meeting rhythms to create new energy and new dynamics and raise attendee enthusiasm. This can involve a variety of things, ranging from changing seats to ditching the seats altogether. However, please note, I am not at all advocating that these alternatives be used 100 percent of the time; doing so would, ironically, turn breaking the habit into a new habit. What I *am* advocating is that meeting leaders be sensitive to rituals becoming ruts, leading to stagnation. A host of ideas for keeping meetings "fresh" and stimulating are presented in the next sections.

The Chair Has More Power Than You Think

Reflect on the last dinner party you attended. Do you remember where you sat? Whether you do or you don't, I can assure you that where you sat at the table directly affected your experience of the event: whom you spoke to, how much you spoke, and maybe even what you ate (e.g., if the mashed potatoes were located at the other end of the table). Table seating matters in meetings as well. Research demonstrates that emergence into leadership positions is influenced by seating location (e.g., it is culturally constructed that the head of the table is a leadership position), and where we sit influences communication flow and whom we are more prone to disagree with. I would argue that even without knowing anything about the individuals in the meeting, a meetings researcher could predict meeting dynamics with decent accuracy by just looking at a photo of the attendees around the table. And, at the same time, we do know that people tend to gravitate to where they sat last. For example, when I teach a class, I can predict with near certainty which seats students will be sitting in on the last day of class (sixteen weeks later) based on where they sit the first day of class. When it comes to seating, we do tend to be creatures of habit.

The dynamics created by seating location do not *necessarily* derail a meeting. But seating can affect meeting effectiveness, critical decision-making, creativity, enjoyment, and energy. Let me illustrate:

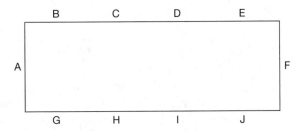

Person A and person F are in privileged speaking locations representing either the head or the foot of the table; they likely will communicate the most given that these positions typically represent leadership roles. This arrangement is fine if their expertise is most important. But if they are misinformed or have bad ideas, their exaggerated influence can be detrimental. Persons C and D will likely have fewer disagreements sitting directly next to one another (e.g., we are more likely to speak and to express disagreement to those sitting opposite us than those directly to our right or left) and may even be more likely to form a de facto alliance of sorts. This is fine if they share similar perspectives. But if their opinions differ, it might benefit the meeting if those differences of opinion are actually discussed—it is often the case that through a discussion of differences a better, possibly synergistic, solution will emerge (i.e., constructive conflict around ideas is a good thing for a meeting). Person J may wind up not participating much in the meeting, especially if person A is the leader. This is fine if person J doesn't really have ideas or much to contribute. But if her thoughts are key to the success of the meeting, this may undermine the meeting's effectiveness.

The takeaway from this seating analysis is not that the meeting leader needs to have a heavy hand in socially engineering the meeting experience, but that having some fluidity in seating is useful so that, over time, a full range of dynamics is experienced in the meeting. This, in turn, serves to prevent pigeonholing folks, helps to keep things fresh and stimulating, promotes different types of communication patterns, and, overall, prevents the meeting experience from becoming stale. The meeting leader can initiate this by simply creating a culture where attendees change seating locations every meeting or at least periodically. Folks will likely grumble—after all, we do gravitate toward predictability—but the meeting leader can just explain that the change is an effort to keep things interesting, stimulating, and "fun." For instance, at each meeting of a board of directors I serve on, our name placards are shuffled and placed in different locations around the conference room. I definitely have experienced the value of this, not only from changing dynamics but also from forming relationships with a greater range of people. Another way for a leader to alter seating arrangements, without people fully realizing it, is to pick different locations, with different table or seating arrangements, for holding the meeting. A change of scenery can be energizing in and of itself.

Somewhat related to the discussion of seating position, I want to introduce another way that a seat can influence the dynamics in a meeting: the use of an *empty chair*. Research on physical cues such as posters and signs suggests that these cues can be effective prompts in influencing a range of behaviors, from the purchasing of goods, to not smoking, to hand washing, to using the stairs. Of course, the cue—like a poster or sign—needs to be salient and noticeable in order to work. In this vein, some companies have implemented the empty meeting chair—an approach that appears to have started at Amazon. This empty chair is a noticeable, physical cue that is meant to symbolically represent the need to recognize the customer in all that is said and discussed. Other companies use the chair to represent other key stakeholders that may not be present (e.g., a supplier). Bottom line: the physical cue of an empty chair can help attendees consider alternative perspectives during the meeting.

The next two techniques, the walking meeting and the standing meeting, throw chairs out the window altogether and provide a different perspective on the topic.

A Walking Meeting

The walking meeting is a mobile meeting designed for two to three, and maybe up to four individuals. We can find many companies embracing the notion of a walking meeting. The biography of Steve Jobs made reference to his passion for taking long walks as a way to have a serious conversation. Other CEOs who use and advocate walking meetings are folks like Facebook CEO Mark Zuckerberg, Twitter cofounder Jack Dorsey, and former president Barack Obama. Walking meetings are a staple at LinkedIn: folks circle around a twenty- to twenty-five-minute looped path in their California head-quarters. It is certainly not just high-profile companies that engage in this practice; this practice can be found at small, medium-sized, and large organizations. This frequent use raises the question: does research support this meeting practice?

Walking is healthy. Headlines abound regarding the health benefits of walking: less heart disease, greater weight control, decreased risk for various cancers and dementia, lower cho-lesterol, and strengthened bones and muscles. Moving beyond physical benefits, research shows a link between outdoor ex-ercise and well-being. *Inc.* magazine reported on an internal study done at Johnson & Johnson on the benefits of walking meetings. Vice president Jack Groppel noted that "in the studies that we did, after 90 days of doing [walking meetings], people felt increased amounts of energy, they felt increased focus, they felt improved engagement."

More energy and engagement should certainly benefit the meeting itself and, in turn, may elevate focus and cre-ativity. With regard to the latter, Russell Clayton, assistant professor of management at Saint Leo University, discusses in *Harvard Business Review* some research he did with colleagues on walking meetings involving one hundred and fifty working adults in the United States. The people in the walking meetings were 8.5 percent more likely to report high levels of engagement. Further, the people who partici-pated in walking meetings reported being more creative at work. Although these observed effects were small, if you take into consideration all of the meetings one person attends, compounded across people and time, even small effects make a big difference.

Furthermore, Stanford University researchers, in perhaps the most rigorous study to date on this topic, examined the link between walking and creativity; the results of this research were recently published in the *Journal of Experimental Psychology: Learning, Memory, and Cognition*. They conducted four experiments examining the effect of walking on creative ideation in real time, but also shortly after the walk. The experiments varied: participants walked inside (on a treadmill) or outside, and these groups were also compared to participants sitting either inside or outside. One of the tasks examined was called the Guilford Alternative Uses (GAU) task. This task asks participants to find alternative uses for common items. For example, in my team creativity workshop, I have attendees generate alternative uses for, say, a paper clip. Creative solutions like a zipper replacement, hair clip, and fishing hook come up. In the Stanford study, walking outside yielded the greatest positive creativity boost across all four conditions. For example, the researchers found that when performing the GAU, over 80 percent of the participants were more creative when walking than when seated, and they were most creative when walking outside. Taken together, it appears that walking is not only good for the individual's mind and body but also results in greater potential for innovative thinking.

Advocates of walking meetings further argue that these meetings enhance meeting outcomes for a variety of other reasons. First, walking meetings can enhance communication in that there is less ability to multitask on the phone or laptop, which results in greater presence and focus. Others contend that walking helps break down formalities, decreases inhibitions, and encourages less filtered communication. In the *Inc.* article mentioned previously, Hiket Ersek, CEO of Western Union, was quoted as saying, "People become much more relaxed, and they talk from their hearts if you go for a walk with them. And they get to the point they want to make much more quickly."

The takeaway from this discussion is not that all conference rooms should be abolished. There are certainly times when projectors, whiteboards, and tables are needed. There are also times when the content of the meeting does not lend itself to a walking conversation (e.g., a disciplinary meeting). Here are some other key usage notes associated with walking meetings:

- Most importantly, walking meetings are really only effective for small gatherings. Two or three attendees is ideal. Four attendees can work with excellent facilitation.
- The agenda must be such that technology tools are not needed. That said, I recommended to one leader that he make voice-to-text memos using his phone, to capture key takeaways during the walk—this is fast and easy.
- Walking meetings are not ideal for conversations heavy on supporting materials or those that require extensive note-taking.
- Remember, these types of meetings still require planning and structure to yield their full potential—you should still have a well-thought-out agenda. They are not just breaks from work.
- If you plan to use a walking meeting, attendees should know this is in advance so that they are not surprised when they arrive (e.g., certain shoes, for example, may not be conducive to long walks). Although comfortable shoes are recommended, the walking speed should be slow and not aerobic in any way.
- Ideally, these walks should be outside; if this is not possible, even a walk inside a building can be a nice change of pace. In either case, pay attention to the route. You want to pick a path that is relatively quiet and circular. If it is not circular, just be sure to end the meeting in an agreed-upon location, such as a coffee shop, the parking lot, or the lunch room.

I'll conclude this section with a passage from a blog by Richard Branson, CEO of Virgin:

> *When given the opportunity I often like to take things a step further—literally, with a walking meeting. I sometimes even set myself a personal challenge of trying to come up with a plan of attack in the time it takes to walk around the block . . . five minutes, go! A lot of time is wasted in meetings. Agendas get forgotten, topics go amiss, and people get distracted. While some circumstances call for workshops and more elaborate presentations, it's very rare that a meeting on a single topic should need to last more than 5–10 minutes. If you stand up, you'll find that decisions get made pretty quickly, and no one nods off! Plus, it's a great way to fit in a bit of exercise and stay focused on a busy day. Another positive about meetings outside the boardroom is a lack of fancy tools, and instead an emphasis on real communication.*

A Standing Meeting

A standing meeting is another way to ditch the chairs and just get up. Here is what we know about *sitting*: too much sitting is bad for your health. It is associated with higher blood pressure, increased cholesterol, and overall elevated cardio-vascular disease. One study, published in the *British Journal of Sports Medicine* and reported widely in the popular press, included eleven thousand adults and evidently found that every hour spent sitting watching TV, DVDs, and other gadgets with screens reduces life expectancy by around twenty minutes. Which brings us to the merits of the standing meeting.

Allen Bluedorn, a professor at the University of Missouri, and his colleagues conducted an experimental study in which they compared standing meetings with sitting meetings in a laboratory setting. They examined a hundred five-person meetings. Although meeting quality was unaffected by meeting format, sit-down meetings took 34 percent longer than standing meetings—so, same quality *in considerably less time*. Attendees also reported greater satisfaction with the standing meetings.

Andrew Knight and Markus Baer, two researchers at Washington University in St. Louis, recently examined fifty-four small groups of three to five attendees. There were two conditions in their study, standing and sitting. The attendees' task was to develop and record a university recruitment video in thirty minutes. Overall, the researchers found that in stand-up meetings there was better collaboration, less possessiveness of ideas, more willingness to consider others' ideas, and greater levels of engagement. Based on this evidence, we can conclude the stand-up meeting is a good tool to have in the meeting leadership arsenal. There are some noteworthy caveats to keep in mind when implementing a standing meeting:

- Be sensitive to meeting length; folks will only want to stand for so long. There is no research on this per se, but I would advocate aiming for fifteen minutes or so. This consideration should mitigate fatigue and prevent any inadvertent privilege of those in good health.
- If you try a standing meeting, keep a close eye on any odd dynamics that might emerge due to differences in physical stature among attendees. For example, you don't want your five-foot, two-inch attendees to feel intimidated by your six-foot, four-inch attendees. Having stools to perch on without a table could be one solution to this type of situation.

Conclusion

The techniques presented here are tools and approaches I encourage you to try—to energize, promote focus, and generally improve the meeting experience. They are just additional arrows in a quiver, tools in a toolbox, colors in a palette, and crayons in a box. Overusing any of these techniques will yield just another habit, so be sure to use them sparingly. Leveraging different techniques at different times, given a set of meeting goals, is a best practice for sure. Trying new things conveys to your team that you care and that you value controlled risk-taking and experimentation. Your team may groan and even tease you when you introduce these alternative methods, but they likely will appreciate that you are taking a banal experience and trying to bring it to life. It only reflects well on you—give it a go. Heed the famous words of William Cowper: "variety's the very spice of life that gives it all its flavor."

Takeaways

1. Humans are inherently habitual. This tendency to favor routines also applies to the meetings we host: they can easily become stale. Our meetings pretty much look quite similar in process, composition, and setup.

2. There are several ways to introduce variety into your meetings; one technique is to change the seating arrangements in your gatherings. Although it may seem rudimentary, whom folks sit next to, across from, and far away from can absolutely affect their meeting experience and the overall meeting quality. As creatures of habit, people tend to sit in the same spots at these meetings over and over again. You can change seating arrangements by simply asking attendees to sit somewhere different, shuffling and placing name placards, or changing the table setup or meeting venue.

3. Another technique to use to introduce some variety into your meetings is having a walking meeting. Research has shown the benefits of walking: everything from reducing obesity and heart disease to increasing creativity and focus. It is important to keep in mind that walking meetings are best for two to four people, they still need to be planned, and, ideally, they should involve an outdoor, circular route (though slight variations on this are welcome).

4. Consider a standing meeting. Similar to walking, standing has health benefits and has been shown to be associated with increases in meeting satisfaction and efficiency. Standing meetings can work for larger groups of people, but they should be shorter—fifteen minutes or so.

Chapter 8
DEFLATE NEGATIVE ENERGY FROM THE START

"You said 'long-story short' 10 seconds ago, seriously, wrap it the f**k up."

Internet meme

Negativity is personally draining and collectively contagious. We know that a person's mood state (i.e., his or her current mood) greatly affects how that person thinks and acts. Not only do mood states vary from person to person, they can vary for the same person over the course of a single day. Mood states may be transient, but the evidence supporting the benefits of positive mood is robust and associated with many favorable outcomes. In this chapter I will discuss how bringing positive energy into your meetings will benefit individuals and teams. Because mood states can be both influenced by and influential on others, the following recommendations are a powerful addition to the meetings toolbox.

Why Positivity?

Positive mood states promote individual cognitive flexibility, resilience, well-being, and even creativity. Interestingly, and of great relevance to this chapter, the collective mood states of the meeting attendees, taken together, also matter. Matthew Grawitch and colleagues from St. Louis University conducted an intriguing study on this topic and published the findings in the journal *Group Dynamics: Theory, Research and Practice*. They used a mood induction process (e.g., having participants focus for three minutes on a recent past event that put them in a good mood, thus prompting that good mood to reemerge to some extent) to create three groups: individuals in good moods, those in bad moods, and those in neutral moods. Groups of meeting attendees in the positive-mood condition outperformed groups in the neutral- or negative-mood condition on a creative task (similar to the paper-clip creativity task I mentioned earlier). The researchers discovered that when attendees were in good moods there was more engagement and a greater likelihood to use and integrate information across attendees. From these findings, it appears that the collective positive mood state serves as an intellectual and social lubricant leading to a more robust, integrative, and creative discussion.

A related study published in the *Journal of Applied Psychology*, conducted by professors and leading scholars Nale Lehmann-Willenbrock and Joe Allen, examined humor in meetings. They videotaped fifty-four actual team meetings in an organization. The researchers focused on patterns of humor and laughter (instances of this were tallied by external evaluators of the videos). The research team was also able to collect performance ratings of the teams by supervisors. In meetings with more humor and laughter patterns (more than would be observed due to chance), there was a greater propensity for socioemotional communication (e.g., support), constructive conversations, and novel solutions. Furthermore, meetings with more humor rated higher on overall team performance. Of course, humor patterns that are more mean-spirited and contain put-down humor, even if they fuel laughter, show a negative relationship with the overall performance of the team.

Unfortunately, I know it may be hard to believe, but attending a meeting does not appear to put people in a good mood. In my early research, I found that meetings are often experienced as a work interruption. We proceed through our workdays engaged in tasks and activities to meet goals and accomplish objectives. A meeting occurs in the midst of these activities. Although most workplaces have many team-based elements, work is largely evaluated individually; individuals are held personally accountable for inadequate performance. Given this, a good amount of our time is spent working on individual-based objectives and goals. While we work, a meeting can break these rhythms. Although we may welcome the occasional interruption, in general, we find interruptions bothersome, agitating, perhaps even downright detrimental to our work and mood. It is not uncommon for negative stress to occur in the face of a distraction; after all, once the distraction is over, the employee must spend additional time thinking about what he or she was working on before the interruption in order to get back on track. Given this, helping folks get in a positive state for the meeting you are about to lead requires a bit of work. First, you will want to do things that help your attendees feel mentally present (e.g., not perseverating about what they were just doing prior to the meeting or what they would rather be doing). Stated differently, to achieve presence and, in turn, positivity, you must start by creating separation from the strain associated with the interruption.

Creating Separation

Even before the meeting gets underway, the leader should actively greet attendees and help folks feel welcome, appreciated, and needed. As a meeting leader, be on your feet, move around to where folks are sitting as they come in. Make eye contact. While the types of greetings will certainly vary depending on relationship dynamics, consider shaking hands, pats on the back as appropriate, and other types of welcoming forms of engagement. If some attendees don't know each other, be active in making introductions and even pointing out common areas of interest. In an earlier chapter, I likened a meeting to a social event, such as a wedding. It should come as no surprise that the behaviors I am describing, as a collective, are examples of what you would expect from a good host. After all, isn't that what a meeting leader is? Above all else, be a source of positive energy. Attendees will immediately feed off your energy and take cues from you about what kind of scene they have just walked into. The research is clear on the concept of emotional contagion: moods travel quickly. As this goes both ways, don't let others negatively weigh you down. Remain upbeat and positive in the face of potential attendee negativity.

As an alternative to greeting attendees as just described, I sometimes use music to foster separation and build presence. I have seen it work wonders. As folks enter the room, have music streaming at a pretty good volume. In fact, I sometimes ask the first-arriving attendee for his or her favorite genre or band and plug it into Spotify. The music can elevate mood in and of itself, but it also serves to punctuate the start of something new. When we reach the designated meeting start time, I turn the music off quite suddenly. This creates an auditory cue that work is now starting. It is an easy but striking intervention to start a meeting.

This advice is designed to set the stage for constructive meeting energy; I will now turn to the importance of *starting the meeting itself effectively and with gusto, and continuing the momentum*. First, meeting leaders must realize that they are uniquely positioned to promote a positive meeting environment. Research has indeed found that the mood of the meeting leader is a good predictor of the eventual mood of attendees. Other work has gone even further: we now know that the mood state of the leader is actually a predictor of group performance. The question now is how can leaders introduce, and more importantly *sustain,* a positive meeting tone and perhaps even create a joyful meeting?

There is evidence that, as the meeting leader, the early social interactions you encourage and promote have the power to influence the remainder of the meeting. For example, a study published in the *European Journal of Work and*

Organizational Psychology examined eighteen newly formed flight crews. The authors did an in-depth analysis of everything the crews said during the preflight phase (which is akin to the very first part of a meeting). First, they found that the types of communication that occurred early predicted the types of communication occurring later for the team (e.g., nonconstructive early conversations seem to persist throughout the meeting). Furthermore, when those early patterns are constructive (e.g., a balanced pattern of interaction), they are ultimately positively consequential to performance. The article concluded by emphasizing the importance of training focused on establishing strong early interactions.

Another study reported in the book *Happy Hour Is 9 to 5: How to Love Your Job, Love Your Life, and Kick Butt at Work (Your Best Self)* is quite intriguing. The author discusses a psychological experiment in which folks were brought together to reach consensus on a contentious subject. But there was a twist. One of the meeting attendees was actually an actor (a confederate) brought in to play a part. The actor was instructed by the researchers to be the first one to speak. In one half of the groups, the actor would say something positive. In the other half of the groups, the actor would say something negative and critical. After this first scripted line, the actor would simply participate in the rest of the group discussions in a neutral manner. What the researchers found was consistent with the flight crew study: early positive comments by the actor were followed by more constructive collective discussions, with increased listening and a higher probability of reaching consensus. When the actor started with a negative comment, however, the discussion tended to be more contentious, the mood was more hostile, and there was a lower probability of coming to consensus. Like playing dominos, how the meeting starts shapes the rest of the meeting. Therefore, it is critical that you start your meeting with intention—with care to ensure subsequent interactions are as positive as possible.

Creating a positive spark to begin the meeting can be simple to do. To start, make your first words to attendees count. Begin the meeting with passion, enthusiasm, vision, and direction. Make it clear why attendees are at the meeting and what needs to get done. Next, a meeting leader can consider using no more than one to two minutes to focus on recognition, celebration, and appreciation—ideally, this is directed at a collective accomplishment, but this can also target individual achievements. This type of acknowledgment and gratitude can build a collective sense of joy and esprit de corps. Alternate versions of this approach (again, just a couple of minutes) also exist, such as going around the table and encouraging each attendee:

- To recognize someone (or the broader collective) who has helped them since the last meeting.
- To recognize the achievement or accomplishment of another person since the last meeting.

A range of other prompts can be asked, of course, as long as they are generally focused on positive topics and don't take too much time. The key is finding the ones you think "fit" with the attendees. However, don't let this become yet another habit. Try using different prompts occasionally to keep the discussion fresh and interesting.

I am also a fan of periodically reminding folks about "meeting values" as a means to further create separation and make early moments positively impactful. As we discussed earlier in the book, leaders should periodically assess the effectiveness of their meetings. One adaptation of this is to ask attendees at some point what expectations they have of the meeting environment—norms and behaviors they want to see in you as leader and in others. This is an ideal approach once a team or task force is created, but it can be used at other time periods as well. See the Meeting Expectations Quick Survey (at the end of the book) that one leader used.

Results from a short survey like this can serve as opening fodder. Namely, if attendees have said that they value and expect, for example, concise input, respectful disagreements, and no side conversation, this can be reaffirmed at the start of future meetings. This does not have to happen at all meetings, but periodically keeping values and expectations alive is a good practice. Doing so helps to build positive and constructive norms and provides the cue that all are starting a new task together, one that has particular behavioral expectations—this helps create separation. Furthermore, we know from research that by making expectations explicit, one increases the chances of them becoming the norm.

Overall, all these various approaches are designed to start the meeting with a better tone than what is typical—a tone where complaints and grousing stay in check.

Tweaking Meeting Processes to Sustain Presence and Positive Energy

As we have seen, starting the meeting in a positive way is certainly important. But a strong start in and of itself is not enough to keep everyone present and deflate negative energy from start to finish. Throughout this book, I have shared a variety of techniques that, besides promoting more constructive and effective meeting processes, are intended to maintain a positive and constructive meeting climate and thus are relevant to this chapter. I want to close the chapter by briefly sharing a variety of additional techniques that, though small in scope, can have positive effects on the meeting and its climate. The various approaches are listed next. I picked seven very different techniques. While these examples are approaches to consider, they are indeed just examples. A meeting leader can dream up and craft any number of potential efforts to draw attendees into a meeting and maintain presence and positive energy. My hope is that these examples help spark innovation and a willingness to try new things.

Offer Food

A meeting leader has at his or her disposal one tool that is an almost fail-safe for creating a sense of separation. It is referred to across the globe as, quite simply, snacks. You may not be surprised to learn that we have consistently found in our research that snacks at meetings are a good predictor of positive feelings about meetings. Not only do people enjoy treats, snacks help build an upbeat mood state and foster camaraderie that can carry into the substance of the meeting itself. A bowl full of a tasty treat, for example, is a small price to pay for a more focused and energetic meeting.

Bring Toys to the Table

Now think of the contents of a child's toy box. Think of those contents laid out on a conference table. Some companies use toys and other items, such as Play-Doh, Slinkys, magnets, and other little puzzles and games, to help create separation and concentration and to foster a positive mood state. There is some research from New York University's Polytechnic School of Engineering that indirectly supports this meeting practice. This work suggests that fidgeting and certain kinds of hand movements can aid in coping with restless energy, stimulate the brain to focus on mundane tasks, reduce stress, and promote overall levels of focus. Plum Organics, a maker of organic baby food and related products, uses a similar approach. It is not unusual to see coloring books actively being used at their meetings. Their chief innovation officer, who was quoted in a 2015 *Fast Company* online article, summed up the company's motivation for this approach: "It's proven that coloring during a meeting helps promote active listening, and is more beneficial than multitasking on something like email."

Establish Technology Policies

Although eating and playing with toys can aid in creating separation and promoting presence, there are some other tangible actions that meeting leaders can take as well. These actions *target technology usage and multitasking*. Over the last forty years, our confidence in our ability to effectively multitask has increased.

The reality, however, is that the human brain has not actually fundamentally changed in these four decades. An unhealthy paradox ensues; we think we are good at multitasking when we are actually not all that good at it. This belief leads us to engage in highly counterproductive behaviors, many of which involve technology. For example, driving and texting has become quite rampant. The National Transportation Safety Board reports that texting and driving is generally the equivalent of driving with a blood alcohol level three times beyond the legal limit. Although it may not be physically dangerous, we also have an issue with using technology while engaged in real-time face-to-face inter-personal interactions. This type of multitasking can undermine active and empathetic listening, lead to distraction, and under-mine the ability to be "present." Furthermore, it can serve to dis-tract those around the multitasking individual and lead to feelings of frustration and disrespect. The solution to these problems is an obvious one: create technology-free meeting zones.

The research supports this solution. Three professors from the Marshall School of Business at the University of Southern California conducted research on perceptions of civility in the context of mobile phone use in meetings. Surveying over five hundred professionals, the conclusions were quite robust:

- Eighty-four percent of respondents said it is rarely/never appropriate to write and send texts or emails during meetings.
- Fifty-eight percent of respondents said it is rarely/never appropriate to even check time with a phone during meetings.
- Older professionals, especially those with higher income levels, reported even lower tolerance for the use of tech-nology during meetings.

Given these results, many companies are banning techno-logy at meetings and asking attendees to check their phones at the door or deposit them in a basket (granted, exceptions exist for employees "on call" or the equivalent). The highest-profile example of this practice is former President Obama's Cabinet meetings, where the use of cell phones was banned so that staff could be entirely present during the meeting. There are a couple of important caveats to this advice. First, banning technology works best if the meetings are short and focused. If the meeting is on the longer side (e.g., an hour or maybe even less), you may want to build into the agenda a technology break so folks are able to check in and quickly resolve issues using their devices. And let's be realistic: given the various levels of technology addiction in our society, this will also likely provide meeting attendees with some peace of mind.

A common question asked when discussing this intervention is whether the technology-free zone should extend to laptops. In general, the answer is yes. Laptops can be just as distracting as phones. Certainly, you can imagine some exceptions to this rule (e.g., attendees who may have meeting-critical info on their laptops). To add to this, an interesting study conducted by psychologists Pam Mueller and Daniel Oppenheimer found that students taking notes by hand, instead of with their laptop, had a significantly better understanding of concepts presented during the class. So, besides decreasing distractions, not using a laptop during the meeting can result in better and deeper comprehension of what was discussed.

Consider Clicker Quizzes

Clicker quizzes are a way of collecting data and opinions during the meeting via an attendee's personal phone or device. The information is instantly collected, summarized, and presented in real time on a display in the meeting room. This technology (e.g., Socrativ) is easy to navigate and there are plenty of instructional YouTube videos for anyone who may need a little help. The process typically involves attendees visiting a website and entering login credentials. Then, a question is put on the screen for attendees to respond to, and within moments the data are collected and results are presented. This is a terrific way to generate high levels of participation in a very efficient manner. The types of questions asked can be closed-ended, such as "Which of the following plans do you want to discuss?" or "Please rate the quality of an applicant for a particular position." The questions can also be open-ended, such as "Please identify any concerns you have about the proposed plan." These quizzes can be easily created in advance of the meeting. However, in the event of an emergent issue or topic that warrants attention, questions can be created in just a few minutes during a quick break as part of a meeting. Although I have not seen any research on using clicker quizzes in meetings yet, I have been completely impressed by attendees' positive reactions to them. Clicker quizzes can promote engagement and focus throughout the meeting, while also adding in a bit of positivity and fun—which, hopefully, you have been promoting from the beginning.

Consider Role Playing Beyond Just Devil's Advocate

Asking someone to play the role of devil's advocate (i.e., a contrarian) can be useful to generate critical thinking. However, there are additional roles that can be assigned as well, depending on the agenda at hand. Most notably, certain individuals can be asked to role play a particular stakeholder not present at the meeting but relevant to the agenda item (e.g., an elderly customer). When playing the role for a certain limited amount of time (five to fifteen minutes), the attendee should be asked to be realistic and engage normally (the person is not asked to dominate the conversation) in the meeting discourse while taking on this other vantage point (roles can be rotated). A process intervention such as this tends to be intellectually stimulating and mitigates ruts and gaps in thinking, and of most relevance to the themes of this chapter, these interventions serve to add energy, engagement, and spice to the meeting.

Get Attendees Talking in Pairs

Before kicking off an all-attendee discussion on an agenda topic, ask folks to get into pairs and talk about the issue at hand for a short amount of time (e.g., three minutes). Then, move into that all-attendee discussion. Although you can have the pairs report their preliminary thoughts to the group, this is actually not essential. In studying and applying this technique for twenty years, I have seen that even when there is no reporting out, participants are still more primed to think about certain topics, and a diverse and robust conversation ensues. This simple action serves a number of purposes. First, it gets everyone involved (e.g., it's hard to sit back and let other people talk in a one-on-one). Second, it gets a host of new ideas on the table, thus helping to mitigate groupthink. Third, it makes it easy for shy people to engage in the meeting in a way that is comfortable for them; in fact, it is often the case that their "partners" become advocates for their ideas. One key to making this process work is to emphasize to the pairs that everything they do in the breakout conversation is just tentative and they are not seeking to come to any resolution (a short time allotment also helps emphasize this reality).

Consider a Good Old-Fashioned Stretch

This one does not require much explanation. It is simple to do and it works well. Periodically, between key agenda items, consider having everyone get up and do a big stretch by reaching to the sky or down to the toes. Ten seconds is all you need to boost energy.

Conclusion

You only have one try to create a good first impression. Those first moments you meet someone are important to get right. The same applies to meetings, especially as people bring a set of baggage with them to the meeting. Whether that baggage is an overall negative feeling about meetings or the feeling of being haunted by a pressing task they are working on independently, the meeting feels like an interruption. As meeting leaders, we need to be aware of this baggage, as it can weigh meetings down and create a negative meeting dynamic that is counter to creativity, constructiveness, and enjoyment. We can actively mitigate these forces by starting and running the meeting in a way that promotes a sense of presence and positivity and, most importantly, honors the time the attendee is investing.

Takeaways

1. Emotions are contagious, and meetings are not immune to this phenomenon. Scholars have shown that positive and negative mood states can spread among meeting attendees; leaders are in a unique position to influence the mood of the meeting.

2. In order to create a positive mood and meeting experience for attendees, leaders should deliberately create a separation between what attendees were doing before the meeting and the meeting itself. There are several techniques for doing this, including intentionally greeting attendees, offering snacks, and playing music as they enter.

3. Another important technique for creating that meeting separation is discouraging multitasking during meetings. In fact, some companies have eliminated cell phone, electronic tablet, and laptop use in meetings altogether; remember, we are not as good at multitasking as we think we are.

4. In addition to creating meeting separation, it is also important to start the meeting on the right foot. Make sure that your opening statement is purposeful, that you consider recognizing group accomplishments (or individual ones), and that you remind your attendees of the "meeting values."

5. Finally, it is helpful to try different approaches, such as incorporating clicker quizzes, encouraging advanced role playing and partner discussions, and even stretching; I firmly believe these techniques promote good energy and mindfulness throughout the meeting.

Chapter 9
NO MORE TALKING!

"The single biggest problem in communication is the illusion that it has taken place."

George Bernard Shaw,
Nobel Prize–winning writer and critic

Remember Life Savers' soda, Bic's disposable underwear, Harley Davidson's aftershave, and the McDonald's Arch Deluxe? Each of these products failed quickly. A dramatically failed product launch from a large company—with such talented staff, so much investment, and so many preparations—is difficult to fathom. Here is another example: how was it possible that Coca-Cola could not anticipate the strong negative reaction to ditching traditional Coke for "New" Coke? After all, they built a business on fostering brand loyalty. Research and case studies suggest that the problem in so many of these decision-making fiascos was that unique, discrepant, and important information did not come up in meetings. Therefore, despite countless meetings to prepare for these launches, critical factors remained under the surface, all but assuring ultimate failure. One key to preventing this outcome: *less talking and more silence.*

Let me start at the end of the story: sometimes it would be incredibly helpful and productive if meeting attendees would just stop talking for an extended period of time. As crazy as it might sound on the surface, there are a host of techniques that cultivate silence to create dynamic, engaging, and rich meetings. Silence can be golden, especially for generating and evaluating ideas in meetings. In this chapter, we will review the case for silence as a panacea for many meeting ills.

The Whole Can Be Better Than the Parts

Although sharing information and coordinating people are clearly utilitarian reasons to meet, there is a greater hope for meetings. There is a hope that when you bring people together to work on a challenge or a vexing problem, something unique and synergistic happens, whereby the meeting outcome exceeds what would have been achieved with a series of one-on-one conversations and emails. Ideally, the interactions among attendees yield ideas and solutions that no individual alone can derive. In organizations, this can be experienced as that "aha moment" when the team surprises itself by coming up with a completely unexpected idea. This is even easier to see in sports—think of an overachieving team that outperforms a set of individual talents—for example, the very young 1980 US Olympic hockey team beating the stronger, more seasoned, and more talented Russian juggernaut team.

Drawing from the research on meetings, a synergistic effect occurs roughly 10–15 percent of the time. While this strikes me as an alarmingly low rate, it is at least clear that the potential for meetings to achieve the unexpected *does* exist. This might mean more and better ideas, richer feedback, insightful critique, and unique integrative paths forward. Most of these, however, depend on the engagement and involvement of the attendees. Perhaps most importantly, for good things to happen, the meeting must tap into each attendee's relevant and critical knowledge, insights, and perspectives. If attendees don't share key information and insights relevant to the meeting goals, especially information they hold uniquely, the meeting is destined for mediocrity, at best. Or, as with New Coke, it can lead to a slew of poor initiatives and product launches.

This leads us to the key question: do attendees actually pass along critical and unique knowledge relevant to the meeting goals? Professors Garold Stasser and William Titus conducted an experiment on the topic of information sharing in meetings—*does it actually happen?* To answer this question, they created a scenario in which each meeting attendee, prior to the meeting, was given information that pertained to a task at hand. Some information was common across all attendees, and some was unique to a particular attendee. The intriguing part of the study was that if attendees pooled together the unique information, they would yield the optimal decision; without all the available information, their decision would miss the mark. A good way to illustrate the sort of task they used is to imagine a hiring committee coming together to evaluate two job candidates after conducting extensive interviews and screenings and checking references. Let's call the candidates "Ms. Gold" and "Ms. Take." If attendees pull all of the unique information from each person, they should realize that Ms. Gold is, by far, the better candidate, based on her credentials, and therefore she should be chosen. But if they focus on information that is mostly shared or common among all attendees, Ms. Take would receive the support; what is special about Ms. Gold, the information only some people have, would remain under the surface. Sixty-five additional research projects later, involving a host of researchers, more times than not what happened was that the attendees discussed the shared knowledge and based their decision on the shared knowledge. The unique information, even when highly relevant, did not bubble up. As a result, in these studies, meeting performance and meeting solutions were often flat and uninspired. Stasser and Titus found in one study, for example, that the superior decision was derived less than 20 percent of the time—in our example, this would mean Ms. Take got the job the vast majority of the time.

Why does the shared information dominate discussion and unique information stay buried? When we present shared knowledge, it is reinforced by others in the form of social approval. Nods, supportive glances, and smiles are common reactions we receive (and relish) when we present information that others believe is true. Shared knowledge does not rock the boat. Unique knowledge, on the other hand, can do just that, as it may serve to challenge ideas and thinking, which is essential to avoiding groupthink (the phenomenon that a group's desire for harmony leads to the pressure to conform and to a lack of critical decision-making). In fact, one of the key tactics known to prevent groupthink is to make sure contrarian and unique perspectives surface during the course of discussions. Reflecting on the failed Bic underwear example, what Bic really needed was a meeting in which attendees voiced concerns, such as (1) disposable fabrics are not very comfortable, (2) is this product really needed?, and (3) does our strong image as a pen company truly position us to pursue this underwear initiative? It is clear: for organizations, getting relevant unique and contrarian perspectives to the forefront is critical.

Could silence actually be a solution to this problem? Imagine the following scenario: Six people are in a room brainstorming solutions to a dilemma. When the brainstorming is done, researchers identify how many ideas were generated and they assess the quality of those ideas. Now imagine six different people in a room, generating ideas on the same problem but in a noninteractive manner—recording their ideas on paper. Upon completion, researchers once again identify the number of ideas generated and the quality of the ideas. Over eighty studies have been conducted using this or similar types of situations, with remarkable results. The participants who interacted during the meeting produced significantly *fewer and lower-quality* ideas than the non-talking meeting participants. These effects became larger and larger as meeting size increased.

Three reasons are offered to explain why the non-talking meetings performed better than the talking meetings for brainstorming. First, there was an absence of "production blocking." In a meeting, the general rule of thumb is that only one person can speak at a time (despite the fact that we often talk over each other). This creates some speaking logjams where ideas are at risk of being forgotten or tabled because an attendee no longer feels they are relevant or needed by the time this person has the opportunity to speak. Furthermore, finding that speaking window of opportunity can prove challenging. Leigh Thompson, a management professor at Northwestern University, found that only a few people do 60–75 percent of the talking in traditional brainstorming meetings. This dominance leaves little time for others to get their ideas in.

A second reason is that attendees who silently wrote down their ideas did not fear social humiliation, especially when written contributions were de-identified. They could contribute freely. Early content shared by others did not frame their reality or create norms around what were socially acceptable ideas and what were not—the table was entirely clear for whatever the attendee wanted to serve up.

The third and final reason is that the silent writing meetings fostered a process in which all attendees had to participate— the paper and pen were directly in front of them. Thus, an attendee could not hide behind others' contributions. Overall, a written silent discussion seemed to reduce the risk that great ideas lay dormant and undiscovered.

As meeting leaders, we must do what we can to capitalize on the critical, unique, and important ideas of our attendees in an effective and efficient manner, because what is the point of bringing folks together if we don't? There are techniques, leveraging silence, we can use to help with this.

A Quiet Path Forward: Brainwriting

Brainwriting represents a series of techniques that strategically use silence to generate ideas and to prioritize ideas. Essentially, brainwriting involves silently sharing written ideas in meetings around a particular topic. Attendees participate in parallel and so there is no need to take turns. Unlike most meetings, where individual contributions are readily apparent, there is a level of anonymity in brainwriting. It is not necessary to include names or identifiers on what each person writes. Additionally, to carry out brainwriting, a facilitator is needed, and the meeting leader does not necessarily need to be that person. The core role of this facilitator is to manage the simple brainwriting process. The facilitator also reminds people of the need for silence during the process. All attendees must respect the silence, as side conversations will derail the process. That said, the meeting leader or facilitator can call silence off at any point, but the key is that it is officially called off for everyone.

The data on brainwriting and its related forms really are quite positive. When implemented, the range of content generated, as well as the satisfaction and participation levels, is an indication that people like it and that it works. One recent study found that brainwriting groups produced 20 percent more ideas and a whopping 42 percent more original ideas as compared to traditional brainstorming approaches. Brainwriting can take on a number of forms, depending on specific need. I will share a few versions just to illustrate the range of options, but each can be adapted further to achieve meeting goals. What they all have in common is their potential to yield tremendous amounts of unfiltered ideas and thoughts in a way that does not compromise peace and goodwill.

Simplified Brainwriting with Voting

This version of brainwriting is as simple as you get, but still impactful. All you need is a pen and paper (loose-leaf sheets, index cards, or even large Post-it notes). Then all attendees gather together. Each person in the meeting is asked to neatly respond to a prompt on a piece of paper. The prompt is a key question, tied centrally to the meeting goal. Here are some examples organizations have used:

- What are one to three key things we can do to improve cross-functional communication?

- What are one to three key things we should do to improve our vendor procurement processes?
- What are one to three key things we should do to improve how we on-board new employees?

The questions are answered by each person, in writing and in silence. Thus, individual responses are not tainted by others or their responses. Only one idea is put on each piece of paper. So, if you have ten people in the meeting, each coming up with three key things, you will have thirty pieces of paper. A small variation of this procedure is to encourage attendees to interact with written ideas so as to create more ideas. A brainstorming prompt is distributed to attendees. However, it is open-ended in nature (e.g., don't just identify one to three ideas; come up with as many ideas as you can to accomplish x, y, z, etc.). Once again, only one idea is put on each piece of paper. Each idea is placed in the middle of the conference table, face down. Then, after participants have run out of ideas, they reach into the middle of the table and draw pieces of paper with new ideas listed. Perhaps reading those ideas will inspire new ones, perhaps not. Regardless, participants can keep drawing papers from the middle and returning them as needed to see if or what inspiration surfaces.

The responses are collected by a facilitator (or two, or three, or four) who sorts responses into piles of conceptually similar ideas (this could take place after the idea-generation meeting or during it). For example, thirty ideas may be boiled down to anywhere from three to ten themes (aka "buckets") of similar ideas. Once the buckets are created, the group is ready for the next phase. In the event the group is left with a small number of buckets, the group could choose to discuss and flesh out each bucket in this or future meetings. Alternatively, leaders can use a voting process for whittling down the number of buckets needing to be discussed. In this case, the facilitator posts the five to ten buckets of ideas on the wall using tape or pins. Each person then considers the top priorities to be worked on. This voting can occur one person at a time, with others' backs turned for complete anonymity, or—at the other extreme—as a free-for-all, where everyone just goes up and places their marks (or stickers) on the ideas they want to see pursued. Votes are tallied and the top x number of ideas or priorities are identified for future discussion and exploration. This dramatically narrows down future ideas to be discussed, in a very inclusive and democratic fashion. The entire process is noteworthy for being inclusionary, engaging, time-effective, and generally free from pressures to conform. These meetings can often take a third of the time that traditional brainstorming meetings take.

Brainwriting with a Written Discussion

Brainwriting with a written discussion takes the techniques just discussed up a notch by fostering a highly inclusive discussion, but doing so entirely in writing. Let's say a team of individuals meets to consider or evaluate a set of five to ten concepts or ideas. For example, I have seen this applied to a meeting evaluating five advertising campaigns, or a meeting evaluating seven ideas for a new employee training program, or a meeting evaluating three ideas for a new product concept.

Each idea or concept goes on pieces of poster paper, which are then taped to the wall or to various tables in the room. They will typically be spread out so as to provide some level of comfort and privacy once the brainwriting process starts. Attendees, armed with pens, roam around the room where the ideas are posted, adding comments or thoughts or things to think about for each idea listed. Comments vary in form and nature. I have seen comments ranging from "I love this idea," to "Hey, I think this can work, but we need to keep in mind that what we do in the United States may not work as well for our associates in France," to "Not sure if our customers would actually want this," to a substantive and fairly detailed critique. Participants can also add comments or thoughts in response to a written comment.

If attendees are not inspired to write anything on a poster, that is okay. They just move on and come back to the idea later. As people mingle about the room, it is clear that as the comments and reactions to the comments accumulate, a discussion of sorts is occurring—but in writing. The process ends after it looks like the flow of comments has dried up. Groups can then proceed to sticker voting or to a discussion on how to proceed; the choice depends on the content and needs of the meeting.

Before closing this section, let me share a particularly memorable example of one leader who used brainwriting. This leader chaired an eight-person task force established by the vice president of human resources to design a mentoring program for new hires. The leader wanted to deliver a meaningful solution but was concerned about the ambiguity and generality of the mentoring program's stated mission (e.g., was this for all new hires regardless of position and location; did it apply to internal promotions?). Thus, she wanted to engage her task force in addressing this concern at the very first meeting.

She opted to employ a brainwriting technique. She gave everyone a handful of index cards with the following instructions: "On each index card I want you to write down one question you would want answered by the VP of HR about our scope and mission prior to us starting. After you write the question, put it in a pile on your right." She then explained that each attendee should keep writing questions on index cards until he or she ran out of ideas (extra blank cards were in the middle of the table as well). Once people could not think of an additional question to write, they could then reach over to their left and draw a card that was passed to them. With that card, they could then do one of three things: (1) read it, be inspired to write a new question on a new index card, then pass both to the right; (2) read it, not be inspired, pass it to their right, and then draw another card; or (3) read it, decide they would like to add a small comment or add-on to the index card, then pass it to the right.

The leader commendably decided to not be part of the actual process. Instead, she focused exclusively on managing the process. She made sure the process never felt like it was dragging. She read facial expressions and cues to get a sense of when to push the process along. When the process was complete, a rich set of issues emerged, including who the mentoring program should apply to, types of resources available, past history with mentoring programs, and what prompted the task force charge. She then met with the VP of HR for clarification around the issues generated. The leader and the entire task force were very pleased with the process. Not only did it result in more enriched information on which to build a well-aligned and effective mentoring program, but it also set the tone for future meetings by establishing norms of innovation, experimentation, inclusion, and enjoyment.

Continuing Down the Quiet Path: Silent Reading

The next technique leverages silence in meetings in a unique way—for quiet reading. Yes, simply reading silently is used as a technique to promote meeting effectiveness. It is particularly well suited for agendas involving a proposal of an idea, concept, or initiative. In many organizational meetings, formal presentations are followed by meeting participants' discussion and evaluation of what was presented. Amazon, and, more specifically, CEO Jeff Bezos, questioned the value of this practice—and for good reason. Bezos wanted ideas to be evaluated on their merits and not influenced by the flash, personality, and speaking talents of the presenter. Nor did he want the implicit pressure to be socially cohesive to dictate the choices attendees made in meetings. Ultimately, he wanted to create an idea meritocracy and saw collective silent reading as a key mechanism to do so.

From that, Amazon initiated a pretty standard practice: ideas, concepts, and proposals had to be written down thoroughly. Meetings then began with a silent period of time to read the fully self-contained document (e.g., questions were typically not asked while reading). This could be anywhere from ten to thirty minutes and did not occur in advance of the meeting—it was part of the meeting itself. Specifically, Bezos and his leadership team at Amazon recognized that folks had busy schedules and it was hard to devote time to pre-meeting work. By building this work into the meeting, everyone was placed on the same plane, allowing everyone to have a common experience and, most importantly, be assured that this work was actually done prior to discussion. In turn, upon starting the meeting, everyone was fully prepared. There were no more complaints about certain individuals shirking their pre-meeting responsibilities. The only person who had to prepare extensively before the actual meeting was the written report "presenter."

Writing in advance of the meeting requires the presenter to think deeply and cogently about what he or she is proposing before engaging extensively with others and using their time. These written reports, no more than six pages, generally follow an accepted flow, which includes topics such as the problem at hand, data that bear upon understanding aspects of the problem, proposed solutions, and how the proposed solutions impact customers. Amazon even provides training programs on how to best write these white papers.

After the silent reading period is complete, a vigorous discussion typically occurs. The discussions tend to be deeper than what one usually gets in meetings, as the written document brings to life a very detailed formulation of ideas and rationale. It has much more depth than a presentation. It is not superficial by any stretch. Because people read faster than a presenter can present, the additional content comes at no time cost. Furthermore, reading gives people control over knowledge acquisition—they can reread a piece if they want. This self-pacing helps with comprehension. When passively listening to a presenter, the mind can more readily stray or wander—something more difficult to do when reading.

The bottom line is that reading the document relative to a presentation allows for much more extensive content, with more retention at an efficient pace. This in turn triggers deep dives, debates, and valuable discourse. It is common practice for the most senior manager to hold comments until hearing others' ideas so as not to sway the discussion prematurely. Typical outcomes of the discussion could be a rejection of what was written (e.g., not a priority to pursue right now); a proposal to revise the written document to address a set of concerns and potentially have another meeting; or an acceptance of the document and its plan, schedule, and follow-up activities.

In addition to the process just outlined, a "lite" version of this technique exists. Namely, the silent reading technique can be used for any type of preparation materials and readings; it does not have to be as formal as a white paper. Meeting preparation is simply made during the first part of the meeting itself so that all attendees are fully engaged with the materials and are on common ground prior to discussion. I have not seen research on this per se, but in speaking with attendees after a process like this, early reports were extremely positive.

Putting It Together

Before closing, let's take a step back to put this all in a broader context. Effective meeting leaders recognize that they are orchestrating and designing a meeting experience when they bring folks together. They are stewards of others' time and, as a result, must plan diligently. When all participants arrive at the same time and work interactively on a task—a typical meeting style that takes place millions of times a day—leaders are actually deciding to use a tool. Let's give this tool a hypothetical name: *the simultaneous verbal interaction technique* (aka the SVIT). Quite the wordy name and a horrible acronym, yes, but it helps make the point that a choice has been made to use a particular meeting technique, without even recognizing it.

The SVIT is the most conventional meeting tool of choice. We typically default to it. However, many other compelling tools exist. The more unconventional tools, like brainwriting and silent reading, represent essential alternative options available to meeting leaders as they consider their meeting goals. What differentiates successful meeting leaders from the unsuccessful ones is the willingness to pick the right tool for the job at hand. Effective meeting leaders have an open-mindedness to consider all possible tools given the goals of the meeting. Then, after trying a technique, the leader can reflect and learn. Adapt and grow. And remember, even if a tool works really well, that does not mean it should be used unequivocally for all future goals. But, as meeting leaders, we do have compelling evidence-based options to consider. We know that silence can indeed be golden. As Will Rogers once said, "Never miss a good chance to shut up."

Takeaways

1. It is possible, and certainly ideal, to have a meeting that creates synergistic outcomes. In a meeting with true synergy, the interactions among attendees yield ideas and solutions that individuals likely would not come up with on their own; in these meetings, the whole is greater than the parts.
2. In order to achieve synergy, you can try unconventional methods, such as incorporating silence into meetings. Meetings with periods of silence, where employees are generating new ideas or forming their own opinion of ideas being presented, can be beneficial because they can counteract production blocking, groupthink, and social loafing.
3. One technique for building effective silence into meetings is to include brainwriting. Brainwriting involves silently writing ideas around a particular topic before sharing them in meetings; research shows that it can produce more ideas and increase creativity. In order to introduce brainwriting, have attendees write down their thoughts and ideas in response to a prompt and then sort them, vote on them, or have a written discussion about them.

4. Another technique that builds on silence within meetings is silent reading. The idea with this technique is to have employees respond to a new idea or initiative by silently reading the proposal instead of hearing a presentation; this can then be followed by a meaningful discussion. Silent reading can increase employees' understanding and retention of the new idea, and it can save time by cutting out the presentation and decreasing pre-meeting preparation.

5. Although the traditional meeting involves general discussion and taking turns speaking while going through an agenda, it is important to remember that silence can be golden. Although incorporating silence into every meeting is not necessary, it can be a good tool for managers and meeting facilitators to keep in mind.

Chapter 10
THE FOLLY OF THE REMOTE CALL-IN MEETING

New technologies are having tremendous effects on our meetings. These technologies can be used to (1) make remote attendees present through video or other means (including virtual reality), (2) facilitate instantaneous transfer and discussion of content among attendees, and (3) promote simultaneous creation of new content. Despite these advances, the fundamental nature of the meeting remains unchanged. The core components of a meeting in the twenty-first century are essentially the same as the core components of a meeting back in the nineteenth century.

That said, there is one technology-related meeting situation that does require a different way of running the meeting itself. This is the circumstance in which all, many, or some of the attendees are calling in to the meeting. I am not referring to video-based calling in—I mean the omnipresent practice of phoning in. Despite the constant advances in video-based technology, this type of meeting situation will not be going away any time soon. People are always on the move. They are often not located in the office or at a desk. Thus, participants are not only remote, they are attending a meeting absent visual cues (they cannot see others, and others cannot see them). This creates tremendous challenges.

Remote Meetings Are Primed for Failure

If you ask employees whether they think remote, audio-only meetings are effective, you will hear a chorus of "no." And yet if you ask employees if they like attending meetings via phone, if given the opportunity, you will typically get a chorus of "yes." How can these two positions be reconciled? Actually, our data speak to that. Employees like to attend meetings via phone so they can regain control of their time by multitasking and engaging in other work while the meeting is occurring. This horrible state of affairs (for organizations and leaders, at least) is not at all a surprise. Earlier I introduced the concept of social loafing—an individual's reduction of effort when in a collective. There is strong evidence to suggest that the more anonymous individuals are, the more likely they are to social loaf. The luxury of not being seen is the perfect environment for anonymity. The remote attendees can just blend into the background. A few well-placed comments such as "I agree" or "tell me more" or "thank you" are all that are needed to appear engaged, while in reality the remote attendees are happily taking the opportunity to engage in other non-meeting work. Assuming each attendee invited to the meeting was truly needed, the lack of complete engagement by remote attendees is clearly counterproductive to the meeting.

Let's assume attendees are indeed motivated to engage in the meeting. In a remote, audio-only environment, truly engaging is actually quite difficult, especially with five or more attendees. Without visual cues, the meeting is potentially fraught with (1) people interrupting one another, (2) difficulty finding a communication rhythm and flow, and (3) potential misinterpretations of what was said when visual cues are not present (e.g., sarcasm and motives are harder to detect). On top of all this, background noise coupled with poor connection quality, if present, serves to further undermine the richness of communication and the ability of attendees to coordinate their communications.

Overall, the social loafing and communication challenges just described necessitate fundamental changes in how we lead this common type of meeting. In the rest of this chapter we will discuss special considerations associated with meetings for which some or all attendees are dialing in. The solutions consist of ways to facilitate these meetings and alternative ways to structure meetings of this type (e.g., interval meetings).[1]

Facilitating a Messy Audio Situation

One way to make these types of meetings effective starts with an attempt to get attendees to ditch the telephone for a video-based approach. Upon scheduling the meeting, I suggest asking attendees, if at all possible, to join the meeting in a video-based way (e.g., WebEx, Google Hangout, Skype). Adding in the visual cues works to counteract many of the potential communication and social-loafing problems noted earlier. However, the video-based solution may still not be possible given attendees' travel schedules, access to technology, and the like. Thus, effectively facilitating a meeting that is either fully or partially attended via audio will require extra thought and work. A set of facilitation tips can help with this daunting task (they are mostly relevant to video-based meetings as well). The following pre-, during-, and post-meeting advice is meant to serve as an add-on and complement to the lessons from earlier chapters in the book.

Pre-Meeting Tips

- Consider "banning" the mute button. While not always possible, it is certainly reasonable to ask participants to find a quiet space where they can fully attend the meeting, thus mitigating the need for a mute button. When someone is on mute, multitasking becomes almost a foregone conclusion.

---

1   This chapter is a bit different from earlier chapters in that research on practices to improve these meeting types is not as plentiful. As a result, I am leaning more here on my experiences in working with organizations as well as on practices that can reasonably be inferred from related research.

- Have the phone conference line open early so participants can be sure everything is working properly. Create a norm of everyone checking in prior to the official start time. Lateness is particularly problematic in this meeting modality.
- Choose agenda items carefully given modality limitations. Most notably, recognize that the ability to have meaningful discussion is hampered when the meeting modality is less rich (e.g., lacks visual cues).

During-Meeting Tips

- Take attendance—call roll. Sensitize everyone to the voices of all attendees. Create accountability for being there on time.
- Have a rule that everyone identifies themselves before speaking (e.g., "This is Gordon, my thoughts are . . .").
- Ask attendees for permission to serve as the meeting "taskmaster," which entails being firm about keeping the conversation on track and calling on different people when appropriate. Attendees will most always agree to this, as all know how dysfunctional these types of meetings can be.
- Use people's names as much as possible throughout the discussion. Actively manage conversation flow. Draw remote attendees in (e.g., "Sasha, share your thoughts"). Be an active "air traffic control" facilitator. Keep a tally to be sure all are contributing, as it is easy to lose track in this modality.
- During the meeting, try to direct questions and comments to specific individuals. If only some of your attendees are remote and other are sitting together, actively bring them into the discussion throughout the meeting.
- Have Instant Messenger or related technology in place, not for folks to engage in side conversations but for attendees to notify you during the meeting if they want to speak or to indicate, for example, if you missed something.

- Without visual cues, it is important that you and others speak at a slightly slower speed with occasional pauses. This allows for greater comprehension.
- If you are using a video-based platform like WebEx or Zoom, leverage the technology to enhance the meeting. Use its full functionality to share the screen, present content, create content in real time, and conduct quizzes or tallies if possible.

Post-Meeting Tips

- Ask attendees periodically for suggestions on how to improve the meeting (things to stop, start, or continue doing).
- Look for future opportunities for attendee face time with one another as a way to build trust, foster connections, promote empathy, learn about others, and understand humor styles. This practice can pay dividends for future meetings.

Alternative Structures

If the audio-only meeting is small (around two to four people), strong facilitation should be enough to mitigate against common modality problem areas and challenges. However, as meeting size increases, the need for more substantive structural intervention increases with it. Thus, let's look at an alternative framework for these types of meetings—one that operates under the assumption that remote meeting success (especially when the group is larger in size) is promoted by keeping the meetings short and focused and recognizing that this type of meeting medium must be augmented with other activities to truly produce optimal outcomes. I will illustrate these principles, and their corresponding best practices, by sharing a story of a manager at Siemens—I will call her Sandy—who leads a team of twelve remote employees.

Use Subteams

Sandy keeps most of her phone meetings to around fifteen minutes in length. These meetings are generally used to communicate information about particular issues, lay out problems that need to be addressed, announce strategies, and, at times, do early-stage brainstorming (e.g., generating initial ideas and thoughts). What she does *not* use the meetings for is decision-making, problem-solving, or any substantive activity involving discussion. When decision-making needs to occur, she does that in one of two ways. The first option is to create three subteams, each with four people. These subteams discuss the problem at hand, generate potential ideas, and draft preliminary solutions. They also decide on a representative to represent the subteam. The subteam is small enough that all are able to be engaged (subteams often rotate membership over time). Later, the representatives of the various subteams, along with Sandy, meet to discuss the problem and come to a decision, which is then explained to all the others. This process is akin to representative democracy. All are involved to some extent in the process but meeting sizes are greatly reduced (four or fewer people), resulting in high levels of participation and involvement. The process avoids many of the communication and coordination challenges associated with large audio meetings (e.g., it's much easier to coordinate phone meetings with three to four people than it is with twelve people).

Use Intervals

The second option for decision-making with a remote team is something I call *using the intervals*—working in the time periods between short meetings. I will share another example from Sandy to help illustrate. Sandy has a remote call with her team during which she outlines a problem that needs to be solved by the collective. She also answers questions that folks have about the problem itself. The meeting is just fifteen minutes long. Then, post-meeting, using a basic Google

Docs type of technology that allows for shared input, folks asynchronously brainstorm ideas and approaches to the problem. After a set number of days, the brainstorming ends. Sandy assigns a representative from the team to clean up and condense the document, which is then used for the next phase—prioritizing.

Team members are asked via email to go back and vote on the five ideas they think are the most promising solutions (this can be done anonymously if desired). A twenty-minute remote call meeting is then set up (this is not hard to do since her team blocks off two hours a week for activities such as this). In this meeting, Sandy shares the top vote getters and leads a facilitated conversation in which folks talk about the finalist options on the table and ask questions. Sandy does not try to seek consensus—she recognizes that the dynamics on the phone would not allow that to happen in a truly genuine way. The next day, team members are asked to vote for what they consider the best solution, using an online survey (e.g., Qualtrics, SurveyMonkey). Sandy announces the path going forward and asks three individuals to lead implementation. These three individuals are given latitude to tweak the solution as warranted given any emergent issues.

In this second approach, I appreciate that Sandy recognized the limitations of the remote telephone meeting and built an alternative meeting process that was highly efficient. The total meeting time was just thirty-five minutes, yet she was able to get a huge amount of engagement and buy-in to the ultimate solution. Her team members felt that the process not only respected their input but also respected their time. A key takeaway I want to emphasize here is that a meeting leader can leverage "meeting intervals" to do incredible things, with an actual net savings in time. While this story illustrates how intervals were used for one meeting purpose, the approach can be altered for most any meeting purpose as a means of gathering information and input, reacting to information and input, voting, and prioritizing.

As a related aside, there are data suggesting that breaking a meeting into two or more smaller parts results in higher-quality outcomes. Let me share some information from a classic study in social psychology that touches on this. The researcher had attendees in a meeting make a decision collectively to address the task at hand. They then told participants to make the decision again—clearly an odd request. The researcher left it open for the team to decide what they wanted to do with the second decision and no preliminary feedback on the first solution was provided. Here is the fascinating part. The second solution typically was more integrative and creative than the first solution *and* attendees recognized the improvement. The researchers suggested that breaking a meeting into parts helps counteract a natural tendency in meetings to seek premature consensus. Namely, attendees often rally around the first reasonable solution and ideas generated, often stopping genuine and critical deliberations too early. Breaking meetings into parts may serve to reduce this bias. Interestingly, a *Harvard Business Review* article published in 2004, titled "Stop Wasting Valuable Time," discussed how companies like Cadbury Schweppes and Boeing have put this practice into action—often having one meeting to discuss alternatives and another meeting to make the decision. These companies have found that by separating discussion and decisions, they can yield higher-quality outcomes.

Conclusion

Having spent over a decade researching how to make meetings more effective, I genuinely believe that the remote, audio-only meeting is the most difficult type of meeting to run—at least if you wish to yield a positive outcome. But I also have seen them work well—if the advice in this chapter is applied to a good extent. I can also confidently say that you, as the meeting leader, will derive incredible satisfaction from being able to pull off this extremely difficult situation. The vast majority of leaders do not do this well. And, while the techniques discussed here are essential for an audio-only meeting, they actually can be applied to other meeting modalities and contexts. For example, meeting intervals can be a powerful intervention for in-person meetings as well.

Takeaways

1. Although there are ever-advancing technologies that are being introduced into our meetings, it is imperative that we remember that the fundamental nature of the meeting remains unchanged. Even with sophisticated technology, the meeting is still essentially composed of work-related interactions, occurring between at least two individuals, that have more structure than a simple chat, but less than a lecture.

2. Most of the lessons in this book apply to all meetings, but there is a certain type of meeting that deserves special attention: the remote, audio-only meeting (e.g., conference call). It is important to remember that these meetings encourage social loafing—an individual's reduction of effort when in a collective; they can also be fraught with communication issues, from misinterpretations to awkward flow.

3. In order to avoid the shortcomings of the remote audio-only meeting, the meeting leader in this type of situation needs to be a very active facilitator. The leader needs to keep the meeting on task, encourage everyone to participate (and say their names when they do so), consider banning the mute button to increase engagement, and constantly evaluate how these meetings are going.

4. If the meeting includes five or more people, it is also useful to consider alternative structures. These can include the use of subteams and leveraging meeting intervals.

Chapter 11
PUTTING IT ALL TOGETHER

Meetings are a foundational characteristic of any organization, and bad meetings should never be accepted as an organizational norm. Meetings are a hefty investment. In the United States alone, we spend over a trillion dollars on meetings per year. We should demand a strong return.

A few times in this book, I have cited Andy Grove, former CEO of Intel, who likened stolen time to stolen office equipment. I would hazard to say that there is no single investment that organizations treat so carelessly, with so little evaluation or drive to improve, than meetings. Instead of actively working to mitigate the direct costs and indirect costs (e.g., frustration, opportunity costs), we accept bad meetings as a way of life. We treat bad meetings as just a cost of doing business. At the same time, I disagree strenuously with management guru Peter Drucker's assertion that meetings should be eliminated because they are indicative of bad organizations. Without meetings, it is hard to imagine an organization thriving, innovating, and being agile and resilient over the long term.

Successful organizations, and successful leaders, understand that small, positive changes—say, one meeting every week—can lead to palpable gains for the organization and the health, motivation, and engagement of its employees. By now, you've probably gathered that poor meeting practices run rampant in many organizations. However, the uplifting news is that so much time can be recouped with a thoughtful approach to meetings. Reclaiming a mere 10 percent of employees' time, applied across an organization, will undoubtedly have a positive impact on the organization's bottom line. In this final chapter, I will tie together the lessons in this book and share a last call to action. These take-home points fall into five categories: (1) visualization and anticipation, (2) preparation, (3) mindset, (4) active facilitation, and (5) reflection.

Visualization and Anticipation

Most organizational activities, especially those dealing with clients, receive some level of anticipatory thought and planning. This may be as little as five to fifteen minutes. But still, it is recognized that some amount of contemplation is essential for carrying out an activity effectively and in a manner that honors the time of others. As a meeting leader, if you simply take a bit of time to think through—to visualize—the meeting, the flow, the key needs, and the key challenges in advance, you will improve the chances of ultimate success. Alternatively, you can more actively engage in the anticipation process by engaging in what is called a "premortem" (aka prospective hindsight) prior to the meeting. In this approach, the leader imagines that the meeting has failed and then works backward to ascertain potential explanations for the failure. By using this technique, the leader can plan the meeting event to avoid or allay the problems present in that scenario. This due diligence is so helpful to ultimate success. And, again, it can be just five to ten minutes. These reflections then feed into the next class of advice: preparation.

Preparation

There are a host of decisions that need to be made, and made well, prior to the start of the meeting. These decisions should be purposely made, rather than decided out of habit and tradition. They concern meeting time, agenda, attendees, and the context for the meeting. As I covered in Chapter 4, Parkinson's law states that work expands to whatever time is allotted for it. As you prepare for a meeting, keep this in mind and take the time to conscientiously choose the length of your meeting (based on the goals, agenda, attendees, etc.). As you plan the meeting time and length, do not discount the benefits of an odd length or start time. If this recommendation is too counter to your culture, consider following in Google's footsteps and replace your hour-long meetings with meetings that are fifty-five or even fifty minutes long (or reduce any meeting by five to ten minutes). You'll likely find that cutting these few minutes will reduce lateness and will create just enough positive tension to make your meetings that much more productive.

As we saw in Chapter 5, the meeting agenda is not the panacea that almost all self-help books on improving workplace meetings offer. Specifically, research shows that just *having* a meeting agenda does not result in a more satisfying or effective meeting. In order for agendas to be effective, meeting leaders have to be intentional about them; they need to be thought out carefully and approached with care, like planning an event. Also, keep your agendas fresh! Do not open your go-to agenda Word document, change the date in the upper left corner, and print it out to bring to the meeting. A good tip for making an agenda that is meeting specific— and will also increase accountability—is to ask attendees for items to include on the agenda. Beyond this recommendation, I suggest that meeting leaders place items that have to be covered near the top of the agenda. If you always have status updates at the beginning of the meeting, consider moving that toward the end. In line with ensuring that particular material is covered, contemplate using time allotments. I recommend that they be considered on a meeting-by-meeting basis—they are not necessary for effectiveness, but they have their place. If you've never used them, or have only used them occasionally, try including them. If you have employees who rarely participate, consider assigning them an agenda item to "own" as a way of engaging them and helping to develop their leadership skills.

It seems reasonable to assume that as meeting size increases, effectiveness will increase; after all, you have a greater number of ideas and resources and more brainpower. In Chapter 6, we reviewed some of the evidence that this, unfortunately, is not the case. Having too many meeting attendees typically equates to too many voices, logistical challenges, and even social loafing. Too many attendees can be problematic, but simply cutting people from the roster is not without complication. Employees who do not receive an invitation to a meeting can feel excluded. You can't blame them—as humans we have an innate need to meet, and when we're invited to something, we feel as though we belong. Thus, by cutting down the invite list you may find more than a couple of despondent employees. To solve this problem, determine how many people are needed, then provide nonessential personnel the opportunity to be involved in a more appropriate way. In an attempt to advise on the "right" number of meeting attendees, I first recommend reviewing your meeting goals to determine who the relevant and necessary parties are. When you identify who the key decision makers or stakeholders are for accomplishing each goal, you will have a much easier time making decisions about the invite list. If some people are required for only a short period, consider a timed-agenda approach: invite different groups of employees to a portion of a meeting that is most relevant to them. It is more likely, however, that you will have a number of people you could make an argument for attending, but they are not really needed. Inviting these ancillary stakeholders will in all likelihood result in an overstuffed meeting. For these individuals, instead of inviting them, try a different approach. Consult these ancillary stakeholders before the meeting to get their input—this will lead to feelings of involvement despite their not being invited. At the same time, take excellent meeting notes (including identifying owners of certain post-meeting deliverables) and distribute them to all, including these ancillary folks. The third prong in addressing meeting size is keeping an invitation on the table for these folks to attend future meetings, if desired. My last advice for keeping meetings to a manageable size is to consider "representative voices," where you assign a meeting attendee to represent the collective interests of a group of stakeholders, like a department, who are not invited to the meeting. This person attends the meetings and is accountable for representing that larger constituency, including keeping them in the loop.

In Chapter 7 we established that we, as humans, fall easily into a pattern of habits and rituals. We tend to have meetings in the same room, at the same time, with the same people, in the same chairs, with the same general meeting approaches and processes. This can result in stale meetings. I have provided a number of ways to introduce variety into meetings; one technique is to change the seating arrangements in gatherings. It may seem basic, but whom folks sit next to, across from, and far away from can absolutely affect their meeting experience and the overall meeting quality. As you've likely noticed, people tend to sit in the same spots at these meetings over and over again. Consider changing seating arrangements by simply asking attendees to sit somewhere different, introducing placards, or changing the table setup or meeting venue. If you'd like to get rid of the chairs altogether, introduce some variety in your meetings by trying a walking meeting. The benefits of walking are well established: everything from reducing obesity and heart disease to increasing creativity and focus. It is important to keep in mind that walking meetings are best for two to four people, they still need to be planned, and they should involve an outdoor, circular route (though slight variations on this are welcome). A last recommendation is to try the standing meeting. Like walking, standing has health benefits over sitting. Beyond health, standing meetings are linked to greater meeting satisfaction and efficiency. Standing meetings can work for larger groups of people, but they should be shorter so as to prevent fatigue—fifteen to twenty minutes or so.

Meeting Mindset

The leader's meeting mindset is a key predictor of meeting success. In Chapter 3, I explained the concept of a giver or servant leader; this mindset drives how the meeting leader facilitates the meeting. If you adopt this mindset, you will plan and lead your meetings with the understanding that it is your duty to make the meeting a good use of time and value for all. Conversely, some leaders may choose to derive power from controlling or dominating a meeting; this person often features him- or herself in all discussions and interactions. This takes energy—energy that leaves little bandwidth to actively manage the dynamics of the meeting. With a servant-and-giver mindset, leaders do not use the meeting to elevate themselves; instead, they actively prepare and participate in an effort to facilitate a good meeting experience. The leader manages crucial meeting dynamics: engaging all attendees, asking the right questions, modeling active listening, drawing out input, playing traffic officer, and managing emergent conflict. Such leaders seek to facilitate actively but without foisting their will on others. These actions build trust, safety, and honesty and generate terrific amounts of input, innovation, and buy-in.

All this being said, none of this precludes the leader from being directive and moving the discussion forward when that becomes necessary. With a servant-and-giver leader approach, this process will be perceived as more genuine by the attendees. They will understand that the leader is acting on their behalf and is committed to the meeting's outcome. Overall, the servant leader takes pride in being a steward of others' time, recognizing that this is the path, ultimately, to success.

Active Facilitation

Because meetings can be experienced as an interruption, meeting leaders should work to promote positivity the moment attendees enter the room. There are several techniques for doing this: you can play music or enthusiastically greet attendees. You may find that offering snacks is a more attractive option to achieve this goal. Julia Child *did* say that "a party without cake is just a meeting," but I make no promises that this will elevate the meeting to a party.

Beyond the steps you can take as attendees arrive, it is imperative to start the meeting off on the right foot. Offer a purposeful opening statement, consider some of the prompts I provided in Chapter 8 (e.g., recognizing group accomplishments), and remind attendees of the "meeting values." To encourage mindfulness (i.e., presence) once the meeting is underway, discourage multitasking during the meeting. Some companies have eliminated cell phone and laptop or tablet use altogether. You may find this to be too much. There may be good reasons to allow some technology in your meetings (phones in case of emergency, laptops for notes), but remember, none of us is as good at multitasking as we think we are. To sustain the momentum from these recommendations and to keep things fresh and engaging, it is important to facilitate meetings with variety. You should consider using clicker quizzes, advanced role playing, partner discussions, and even stretching; these techniques promote good energy and mindfulness throughout the meeting.

If you'd like to move beyond more conventional techniques, try incorporating silence into meetings. Meetings with periods of silence, when employees are generating new ideas or forming their own opinion of ideas being presented, can be beneficial because they can counteract production blocking, groupthink, and social loafing. In Chapter 9, I described some techniques for incorporating silence into meetings: brainwriting and silent reading. Brainwriting involves silently writing ideas about a particular topic before sharing the ideas with others in the meeting. Although silent brainstorming may seem counterintuitive to the purpose of meetings, research shows that brainwriting can produce *more* ideas and *increase* creativity. To introduce brainwriting, offer index cards, scrap paper, or even

Post-it notes for attendees to write down their thoughts and ideas in response to a prompt. Sort the ideas, then vote on them or have a written discussion about them. The second technique that builds on silence within meetings is silent reading. With this method, the typical start of meeting, idea or initiative, and PowerPoint presentation are ditched by having employees silently read a proposal (or other discussion fodder). This can then be followed by a meaningful discussion. Silent reading can increase employees' understanding and retention of the new idea and it can also save time by cutting out the presentation and decreasing pre-meeting preparation.

Finally, it is almost inevitable that you will, at one time or another, lead meetings that are not entirely face-to-face. Someone may be traveling or you may be working with attendees who are not colocated. Under these circumstances it is essential to recognize the unique challenges associated with remote meetings and how to overcome them. It is important that you consider alternative ways to structure meetings of this type (e.g., shorter meetings, interval meetings, pre-meeting data collection). Further, be comfortable in fully embracing your role as an active "taskmaster," drawing attendees in by name, asking questions of particular individuals, and considering banning the mute button to reduce multitasking.

Reflection

In Chapter 3, I gave you the bad news: chances are, you're not quite as good at leading meetings as you think you are. Relax, you're in good company. Evidence shows that, across all ages and walks of life, we are likely to overestimate our abilities. Now, we may be equally as good at evaluating our leadership skills as we are at seeing the backs of our heads without mirrors, but in accepting this reality, we can work on self-awareness and making improvements.

When it comes to meetings, there are signals that, if we actually look carefully, inform us about meeting quality and our leadership. Are attendees on their phones throughout the meeting? Are attendees engaging in a host of side conversations? Are attendees reluctant to disagree with one another? These are all negative reflections on our meeting leadership. When we are doing the majority of the talking and attendees are not actively participating in discussion—you guessed it— this is a negative reflection on our leadership. When we get these signals, our attendees are giving us feedback. Needless to say, if these signals are present, change is warranted.

Putting this informal scanning of cues aside, the best practice for leaders is to periodically evaluate their regular meetings. The evaluation should be quick and easy: a survey given to all members containing a handful of questions (e.g., things to stop, start, and continue doing). These data will increase your self-awareness as a meeting leader and give you a more accurate picture than your perceptions alone. Once you receive feedback, you can implement change—the sort of change that will promote effectively facilitated meetings and attendee appreciation for actually caring about them and their time.

The Bottom Line

Poorly conducted meetings clearly hurt leaders, teams, departments, and organizations. The answer is not eliminating meetings. If we eliminate meetings, the organization suffers, as meetings have the potential to serve so many positive purposes. First, meetings allow individual attendees to interpersonally connect with one another, which serves to build relationships, networks, and, most important, support. Second, meetings can be an ideal venue to bring together ideas, thoughts, and opinions—things that should help each person perform his or her job in a better, more coordinated and cooperative manner. Third, meetings enable leaders and employees alike to create a shared understanding that promotes efficiency and teamwork. Fourth, meetings build commitment to goals, initiatives, and broader aspirations that may not be explicitly stated in any individual job description. Employees can see they are part of something bigger than themselves. Finally, meetings bring individuals together as a coherent whole. As a result, this coherent whole can be more adaptive, resilient, and self-directing, especially in the face of crises.

My hope is that, as a meeting leader, you try new approaches, and you experiment to improve your meetings. You need not try everything at once; in fact, you can try just a small number of things and see how it goes. Then, with time, you can add more. And more. Make this an active process. Try, reflect, and learn. Try, reflect, and learn. Not only will you see a direct improvement in your meetings, but the process will communicate to those around you that you are willing to experiment, to take reasonable risks, and to grow. This, in turn, helps build a culture of innovation and success. Furthermore, it will hopefully inspire others around you to do the same with regard to their meetings. Next thing you know, a greater return on the meeting investment is occurring as a broader enterprise. Together we can fix the current dysfunctional state of meetings, one meeting at a time. At the very least, as a meeting leader you can fix the meetings you lead and control.

Epilogue
TRYING TO GET AHEAD OF THE SCIENCE—USING SCIENCE

Throughout this book, I have sought to apply the science of meetings to identify vexing meeting issues and possible evidence-based solutions. In this chapter, we will try to get ahead of the current science by surveying those on the front lines and gathering their ideas and recommendations to improve meetings. This chapter was cowritten with one of my terrific doctoral students, Kelcie Grenier.

What Was Done

I wanted to know what innovations meeting users had seen or experienced that they felt were successful. Using LinkedIn, an email was sent to a large number of professionals inviting them to participate in a five-minute survey on meetings. The survey had two primary questions. They were:

- "Moving away from the basics (e.g., an agenda), what are some of the most innovative things you have seen *A LEADER* do to make their meetings effective?"
- "What are some of the most innovative things you have seen *AN ORGANIZATION* do to make meetings at work more effective and better uses of time (e.g., implement certain training programs; mandate certain meeting-free time zones)?"

We had over a thousand participants complete the on-line survey. The respondents spanned a large variety of job types: CEO, vice president of marketing, quality assurance manager, IT professional, management consultant, nonprofit executive, reporter, kennel supervisor, and so on. The companies the participants worked for were equally diverse: they ranged from Google to Bank of America to a local construction company.

Next, we combined the responses from the two questions about meeting innovations—this yielded around a hundred pages of free-flowing ideas in the participants' own words. As you would suspect, many of the ideas were similar. Using thematic analysis, we were able to boil down the nearly two thousand innovations into forty-eight overarching patterns of advice. These forty-eight pieces of advice could be sorted into four broad categories:

1. Recommendations for meeting preparation
2. Recommendations for how to carry out the meeting
3. Recommendations for closing the meeting
4. Recommendations for needed organizational policies and practices

For each of the four categories, respectively, we created a table to capture the types of recommendations forwarded. We also put an asterisk after an idea if it came up quite frequently. Note, an idea broached frequently does not necessarily mean it is a better recommendation. It just means it came to mind for a large number of participants.

One of our principal motivations for doing this chapter was to identify improvement ideas that the current state of research had not yet uncovered. Interestingly, it appears that the extant research is highly in touch with the success stories of meeting-goers. We were gratified to see that the innovations generated in our survey effort, from the mouths of the end users, were well aligned with what was covered in this book.

RECOMMENDATIONS FOR MEETING PREPARATION

Recommendation	Example from Survey Results	More Information
*Only meet when truly needed.**	Leaders should cancel meetings when the items have already been addressed, when the reason for the meeting can be resolved using alternative methods (e.g., email), and when the needed attendees cannot be present.	Chapters 4 and 5
Invite the correct people.	Invitations are only sent to those who are necessary for the meeting or whose presence would promote their own professional development. Further, trust employees to know when they will not add value. Give attendees the power to voice this and to decline meetings when they are in this position.	Chapters 5 and 6
*Gather input prior to the meeting.**	In order to include attendees in the agenda-development process, send a call for input asking for general comments, thoughts, and what agenda items should or should not be included. Surveys are a particularly effective way of gathering this information.	Chapters 5 and 6
Prioritize items in the agenda and set up time restrictions.	Develop an agenda with items that are prioritized, and have a set amount of time dedicated to them.	Chapters 4 and 5
*Provide an agenda ahead of time.**	Send the agenda to all attendees before the meeting. Include additional information such as the goals for the meeting and the purpose of each participant's attendance.	Chapter 5
Provide limited, but necessary, preparatory materials.	Send any necessary reading or introduction materials before the meeting. Limit the amount of materials when possible.	Chapter 9
*Choose the environment with intentionality.**	Plan the meeting's environment and employ tactics such as standing or walking meetings, using spaces outside the typical boardroom, and potentially assigning seats to promote variety.	Chapter 7

Note: asterisk denotes a topic mentioned frequently.

RECOMMENDATIONS FOR CARRYING OUT THE MEETING

Recommendation	Example from Survey Results	More Information
*Delegate roles to attendees.**	Assign responsibilities to meeting participants (including leading the meeting) and consider rotating the responsibilities on a regular basis.	Chapters 3 and 5
Do what is possible to be sure attendees are on time.	Prohibit disruption associated with late attendees by preventing late individuals from entering and/ or speaking with these attendees individually following the meeting.	Chapter 4
*Leverage technology in order to include necessary employees, even when they are not physically present or colocated.**	Conduct the meeting using a medium that will comfortably accommodate as many attendees as possible. By allowing virtual meetings, attendees unable to be physically present and those who would otherwise travel solely for the meeting can participate with the least amount of disruption to their work.	Chapter 10
*Do not allow the use of personal devices that may be a distraction.**	Do not allow distracting technology to enter the meeting space. Consider checking phones at the door, placing them in a shared basket, or at the very least simply prohibiting them from being used.	Chapters 7, 8, and 10
Use mindfulness techniques to create focus at the start of the meeting.	Start the meeting using mindfulness techniques, even if just for a few minutes.	Chapters 8 and 9
Check in on the attendees as they enter.	Check in with the attendees: ask how they are doing. Show them you have an interest in their well-being.	Chapter 8
Use ice breakers.	Start the meeting by using simple ice breakers. Thought-provoking ice breakers such as "name the best movie and why" can encourage creativity.	Chapters 5 and 8
Offer appreciation.	Begin by expressing appreciation for the attendees' work and contributions.	Chapter 5

Use and display a "cost calculator" to reinforce the importance of time.	Conduct and display a "financial analysis" or "cost calculator" in which the hourly wages of the attendees are used to determine how much the meeting will cost—both to ensure time restrictions are upheld and to determine how necessary the meeting is.	Chapter 2
Encourage active participation.	Use visuals, with the goal of active participation. However, be sure the visuals are not distracting (e.g., limit the number of slides in a PowerPoint presentation). Beyond visuals, use other active-participation techniques, such as role playing.	Chapters 8 and 9. See Good Meeting Facilitation Checklist
Provide or support the use of fidget items.	Recognize and support providing an environment for those who may need some ability to "fidget" in order to better focus. Offer (or at least support) pipe cleaners, modeling clay, fidget spinners, and the like.	Chapter 8
Plan for breaks.	Plan for, and use, short breaks for attendees to use the restroom, get drinks, and check their electronic devices.	Chapters 4 and 8
Use humor.	Keep the meeting lively by incorporating some lightness. Not only will this make the meeting less monotonous, but it has the potential to break tension.	Chapter 8
Lead meetings with questions.	Develop an agenda that consists of questions, rather than statements.	Chapters 3 and 5
*Use technology to allow attendees to contribute and react to others in real time.**	Use programs for screen sharing and shared documents to allow attendees to take notes and conduct work simultaneously.	Chapter 6
Assign participation randomly.	Assuming all attendees are able to contribute to any topic, keep attendees focused and ready to participate by randomly selecting attendees for participation. Websites and applications can be used to achieve this goal without bias.	Chapter 10

*Elicit input from those who may not feel comfortable or may be overshadowed by other attendees.**	Be sensitive of those who may not be the loudest but have input to offer. Actively encourage their participation.	Chapters 3, 5, 7, 8, and 9
Encourage attendees to offer alternative positions.	Play, or encourage others to play, the devil's advocate in some discussions. Create an environment that supports opposing opinions and creative thinking beyond the beliefs and assumptions the participants already hold.	Chapters 3, 8, and 9. See Good Meeting Facilitation Checklist
*Tactfully redirect conversations that are off-topic or otherwise unproductive.**	Identify and use tactful techniques to redirect conversations that are contributing to the goals of the meeting. Use the "parking lot" technique, when appropriate, to come back to topics that would be better addressed at a later time or in another meeting.	Chapters 3 and 4. See Good Meeting Facilitation Checklist
*Stick to planned time restrictions when possible.**	Follow the time guidelines defined in the agenda by starting on time and guiding attendees to a close as the end of the time approaches.	Chapter 4
Recognize contributions above the leader's own.	Encourage attendees to participate, and recognize when the meeting would benefit most from their participation, rather than that of the leader.	Chapter 3. See Good Meeting Facilitation Checklist
Gather input throughout the meeting.	Throughout the meeting obtain feedback regarding what needs to be addressed (and how many have these questions), and vote on ideas to move forward most effectively. Doing so anonymously (using appropriate technology such as clickers) is helpful.	Chapters 8 and 9. See Good Meeting Facilitation Checklist

Note: asterisk denotes an item mentioned frequently.

RECOMMENDATIONS FOR CLOSING THE MEETING

Recommendation	Example from Survey Results	More Information
End the meeting on time.*	Using the agenda and schedule as a guide, be sure to address necessary items, but do not keep attendees beyond the time outlined in the meeting invitation.	Chapter 4
End meetings that have addressed the necessary items.	When meetings have tackled the agenda in full, end the meeting. Do not try to "fill" the remaining time with additional items.	Chapter 4
Assign tasks to individuals such that everyone is in agreement.	Keep a running list of action items (such as in a shared document) and establish consensus and clear understanding of who is responsible for items and what the expectations are (such as deadlines).	Chapter 5
Summarize after the meeting to provide attendees with an opportunity to reflect and recap later.	Send an email to recap the discussion and decisions and to reiterate the action items. Send this document to those present and to those whom the information applies to, even if they were not present at the meeting. Invite attendees to comment if your summary is incorrect in any way.	Chapter 6
End the meeting on a positive note.	Ensure that attendees leave the meeting with a positive evaluation of the process and experience. This may be achieved by offering lunch at the end of the meeting, to encourage relaxed discussion and an opportunity to connect with other participants.	Chapter 8

Note: asterisk denotes an item mentioned frequently.

RECOMMENDATIONS FOR ORGANIZATIONAL POLICIES AND PRACTICES

Recommendation	Example from Survey Results	More Information
*Reduce the length and frequency of meetings, when applicable.**	Set and support standards for meetings that are shorter or less frequent. Allow departments to reassess what these standards should be on a regular basis (e.g., semiannually).	Chapter 4
Develop a late policy that is uniformly applied.	Apply a late policy at the organizational level (such as "those who are late are not able to attend") rather than using a leader-specific policy that varies across the organization.	Not discussed
*Set aside specific times and days that are designed for meetings or for the absence of meetings.**	Mandate times or days when meetings are not allowed, such as "meeting-free Fridays," to give employees guaranteed, uninterrupted time. Further, set aside times or days that are dedicated solely to meetings so that it is easier to schedule meetings that all relevant individuals can attend.	Chapter 4
*Identify and enforce what is considered an appropriately sized meeting.**	Set a standard for what size meeting is supported. Aim for meetings that are smaller and, as described earlier, only include the needed individuals.	Chapter 6
Use huddles.	Use short, frequent huddles to encourage focus or to facilitate interdepartmental updates.	Chapters 3 and 4
*Schedule "odd times" meetings (ten minutes after, etc.).**	Promote a culture of meetings that provides time to travel and gives breaks. Start and end meetings outside traditional thirty- or sixty-minute increments, such as fifty-minute meetings.	Chapter 4
Organization-wide policies and expectations should be available for review by all.	All members of the organization should be aware of, and understand, meeting expectations. This may be executed by having "rules" posted in conference rooms or expectations visually displayed throughout the organization.	Chapter 7

Provide adequate training.	Provide skills training to both those in and those not in leadership roles. Consider the use of simulations, such as those available in some academic programs and online, as an opportunity to train in a more active way.	Chapter 3
Provide leaders and attendees with robust meeting behavior feedback.	Gather feedback with objective, outside observers, and/or attendee assessment. Collect further data by recording meetings. Use this information to inform leader- and organizational-level training and development.	Chapters 3 and 8
Encourage leaders to be innovative and to try new meeting practices.	Use the organization's values and culture as a driving force in establishing and maintaining meeting expectations. Reinforce expectations daily. Encourage innovations, while also embracing the instances in which innovations did not work, and use these events as learning opportunities.	Chapters 4, 9, and 11

Note: asterisk denotes an item mentioned frequently.

Tool
MEETING QUALITY ASSESSMENT—CALCULATION OF A WASTED MEETING TIME INDEX

Instructions: Reflect on your meetings. In this assessment you are asked to indicate the percentage of time that certain "negative things" happen or are present in your meetings. Rounding to the nearest 10 percent is totally fine (e.g., 10 percent, 20 percent, 30 percent). There is no need to overthink a response.

Section 1: Consider the following about the design of meetings (i.e., pre-meeting activity) and indicate the percentage of time it was true for the meetings you had over the last month.

	MEETING DESIGN	% of Time This Occurred
1.	Goals of the meeting were not clearly defined.	
2.	Attendees did not provide input for the agenda.	
3.	No agenda was provided to attendees in advance of the meeting.	
4.	Necessary materials were not distributed in advance of the meeting.	
5.	Not all relevant persons were invited or present at the meeting.	
6.	Too many individuals were invited to the meeting.	
7.	Persons not needed, given the meeting goals, were present at the meeting.	

8.	The meeting room and technology were not conducive to a quality conversation.	
	Total, combined percentages of these eight items	%
	Average percentage of these eight items (divide total by eight)	%

Section 2: Provide ratings about the meeting itself from three perspectives: time dynamics, interpersonal dynamics, and discussion dynamics, and indicate the percentage of time it was true for the meetings you had over the last month.

	THE MEETING ITSELF: TIME DYNAMICS	% of Time This Occurred
1.	The meeting started late.	
2.	Attendees came late to the meeting.	
3.	Attendees did not come to the meeting prepared.	
4.	The meeting leader did not come prepared.	
5.	The time allotted to the meeting was more time than was actually needed.	
6.	Time was not used effectively in the meeting.	
7.	The meeting felt rushed.	
8.	The meeting ended late.	
9.	The meeting was not really necessary.	
	Total, combined percentages of these nine items	%
	Average percentage of these nine items (divide total by nine)	%

	THE MEETING ITSELF: INTERPERSONAL DYNAMICS	% of Time This Occurred
1.	The diverse perspectives of attendees were not taken into consideration.	
2.	Attendees did not seem to really listen to one another.	
3.	Some attendees dominated the meeting at the expense of others.	
4.	Disagreements among attendees were counterproductive.	

5.	Attendees did not treat each other with respect.	
6.	Attendees did a lot of complaining.	
7.	Attendees were not open to new ideas or thinking.	
	Total, combined percentages of these seven items	%
	Average percentage of these seven items (divide total by seven)	%

	THE MEETING ITSELF: DISCUSSION DYNAMICS	% of Time This Occurred
1.	Attendees seemed to hold back their candid thoughts.	
2.	Attendees were not encouraged to participate.	
3.	Attendees rambled on and thus did not move the discussion forward.	
4.	Discussion strayed into irrelevant topics.	
5.	Distracting side conversations occurred among small groups of attendees.	
6.	Attendees multitasked during the meeting (e.g., were on their phones).	
7.	Meeting attendees were not engaged in the meeting.	
8.	Critical and thoughtful decision-making did not occur.	
	Total, combined percentages of these eight items	%
	Average percentage of these eight items (divide total by eight)	%

Section 3: The following concerns activities at the end of the meeting or in response to the meeting. Indicate the percentage of time it was true for the meetings you had over the last month.

	POST-MEETING	% of Time This Occurred
1.	When the meeting ended, it was not clear what the action items were and who was responsible.	
2.	When the meeting ended, there was no effort to summarize what was resolved and decided on.	
3.	The leader did not follow up on what all were supposed to do.	

4.	Attendees did not follow up on what they were supposed to do.	
5.	No effort was made to evaluate the quality of the meeting.	
	Total, combined percentages of these five items	%
	Average percentage of these five items (divide total by five)	%

Now let's calculate a grand average percent by plugging in the average percentages above.	
MEETING DESIGN	%
THE MEETING ITSELF: TIME DYNAMICS	%
THE MEETING ITSELF: INTERPERSONAL DYNAMICS	%
THE MEETING ITSELF: DISCUSSION DYNAMICS	%
POST-MEETING	%
Total, combined percentages of the five categories	%
Grand average percentage of the five categories (divide total by five)	%

The grand average percent that is calculated represents *wasted meeting investment*—a wasted-time index. Here is a guide to interpret your grand scores based on my work with organizations:

- If your scores are between 0 and 20 percent wasted meeting investment, your meetings are really quite productive. While there is room for improvement, your scores are above what is typical.
- If your scores are between 21 and 40 percent wasted meeting investment, your meetings are generally hit or miss. Plenty of time is being wasted. Improvements need to be made, but your scores are (sadly) typical of what we find in organizations.
- If your scores are above 41 percent wasted meeting investment, your meetings need substantial improvement. Your scores are considerably below average.

Tool
SAMPLE ENGAGEMENT SURVEY AND 360-DEGREE FEEDBACK QUESTIONS ON MEETINGS

Engagement Survey Sample Questions

Questions can focus on the quantity and quality of meetings within a team, a department, an enterprise, or all of these. Or, questions can focus on meeting effectiveness skills and behaviors for various leaders (and even peers). Some examples of survey items, which are answered using a response scale of "strongly disagree" to "strongly agree," are as follows:

- My supervisor runs meetings effectively.
- My peers run meetings effectively.
- In reflecting on the meetings in my department, I would generally describe them as being engaging.
- In reflecting on the meetings in my department, I would generally describe them as being well run.
- In reflecting on the meetings in my department, I would generally describe them as being necessary and needed.
- Our meetings contain only those individuals who truly need to be there.

360-Degree Feedback Sample Questions

Questions can focus on how the focal person is doing overall in leadership of meetings or can focus on particular meeting behaviors. Again, these can be answered on a response scale of "strongly disagree" to "strongly agree." Some examples:

Colleague X

- Runs meetings effectively.
- Provides an agenda in advance of the meeting.
- Asks for input on the agenda prior to the meeting.
- Documents action items and follows through on these commitments.
- Uses meeting time to address critical issues.
- Keeps discussion flowing.
- Covers relevant issues at meetings.
- Encourages attendee participation at meetings.
- Maintains an environment in which people are comfortable disagreeing.
- Listens carefully during meetings.
- Does not allow any one individual to dominate the meeting.
- Plans the meeting carefully.

Tool
GOOD MEETING
FACILITATION CHECKLIST

Time Management

- Keep track of time and pace the meeting effectively given the big picture of the agenda. Be willing to call a break, if needed, to regroup or if energy is waning.
- Do not rush through an emergent issue that truly needs to be discussed. Be able to recognize if an issue raised is best addressed at a subsequent meeting.
- Keep conversation flowing (e.g., recognize a tangent and pull it back into what needs to be discussed).

Active Listening

- Model active listening as others speak (e.g., really understand what others are saying). Ask excellent questions so that ideas are truly understood.
- Keep clarifying and summarizing where things are and people's input so that everyone understands the process and the discussion at hand.
- Listen carefully for underlying concerns and help bring them out so that they can be dealt with constructively.
- Keep engaged with the note-taker so that issues, actions, and takeaways are recorded and not lost. Confirm with the attendees that all is correct.

Conflict Management

- Encourage conflict around ideas (e.g., any concerns with this idea), and then actively embrace and manage the conflict so that benefits for performance and decision-making ensue (e.g., here is where folks are aligned, here is an issue that we should speak more about). Immediately stomp out negative personal attacks and bring the group back to the need for constructive discussion of ideas.
- Maintain an environment where people are comfortable disagreeing (e.g., thank people for sharing divergent points of view). Invite debate.
- Deal with disrespectful behavior quickly through re-direction, comments about staying constructive, and reminding attendees of the meeting ground rules.

Ensuring Active Participation

- Actively draw out input from others (e.g., asking those who have not yet contributed to share their thoughts). Keep mental track of who wants to speak and come back to them.
- To keep an attendee from dominating the conversation, use body language (e.g., a subtle and small hand movement to indicate the need to stop speaking) and transition statements (e.g., "thank you for that").
- Keep side conversations at bay by reigning folks' comments in.

Pushing for Consensus

- Test for agreement and consensus to get a sense of where attendees are at, but do not unduly and unnecessarily pressure others to reach a conclusion when not ready (unless there is a time urgency).
- Be willing to take the pulse of the attendees to be sure the process is working and leading to excellent decision-making.

- Know when to intervene assertively in the meeting process and provide direction (e.g., the group lacks focus and is talking over one another) and when to let the process run as it is.
- Be an honest broker of the conversation at hand, not privileging your viewpoint or ideas in the discussion. Work to remain impartial. Make it clear that your opinion is just one opinion to be discussed.

Tool
HUDDLE IMPLEMENTATION CHECKLIST

Common Huddle Topics (Pick One to Three)

What Has Happened and Wins	**What Will Happen**
• What did you accomplish since yesterday? • What did you finish since yesterday? • Any key wins for you or for the team that you can share? • Any key client updates?	• What are you working on today? • What is your top priority for the day? • What is the most important thing you will get done today? • What are your top three priorities for the day or the week?
Key Metrics	**Obstacles**
• How are we doing on our company's top three metrics? • How are we doing on your team's top three metrics?	• What obstacles are impeding your progress? • Any "stuck points" you are facing? • Any roadblocks the team can help with? • Anything slowing down your progress?

Huddle Implementation

When, Where, and How?

_____ Is ten or fifteen minutes in length

_____ Occurs at the same time each day (or every other day)

_____ Is best done in the morning

_____ Occurs in the same place, typically

_____ Often occurs standing up, if possible

Keeping Things in Line

_____ Start and end on time
_____ Remind everyone about the goals of the huddle and why they are being done
_____ Create huddle rules (e.g., succinct communication)
_____ Remind people of huddle rules
_____ Create "magic time" when rollover discussion occurs
_____ Evaluate periodically

Involvement

_____ Invite others to provide input into the huddle design
_____ Usually involves the same people
_____ Attendance is generally mandatory
_____ If folks can't attend in person, they attend remotely
_____ Be sure all attendees are talking to each other, not just the leader
_____ Rotate leadership occasionally

The Last Ingredient

_____ Try to have fun with huddles

Tool
AGENDA TEMPLATE

AGENDA
MEETING DATE: MEETING TIME: LOCATION:
Major goals for the meeting (or key decisions that must be made)
1.
2.
3.
Item 1:
Description *Process note*: *Preparation*: *Time (if applicable)*:
Item 2:
Description *Process note*: *Preparation*: *Time (if applicable)*:

Item 3:
Description
Process note:
Preparation:
Time (if applicable):

Item 4:
Description
Process note:
Preparation:
Time (if applicable):

Wrap-up:
• Key takeaways from meeting • Actions and responsible individuals • Notes about next meeting (perhaps topics to cover)

Tool
GUIDE TO TAKING GOOD
MEETING MINUTES AND NOTES

- ☐ Write down important facts and takeaways, including who, what, when, and where.
- ☐ Record key decisions or action plans made in the meeting.
- ☐ Record any questions raised and their answers, as well as ideas provided by the team.
- ☐ Develop a shorthand for taking notes quickly. Consider using a note-taking software (e.g., Google Docs) that multiple attendees can contribute to at once. This keeps participants engaged.
- ☐ Focus on important points. Don't record small talk or info that doesn't benefit anyone.
- ☐ Agree on who will take notes. Consider rotating this responsibility or assigning multiple note-takers.
- ☐ The note-taker shouldn't be someone who runs the meeting.
- ☐ Include the date, a list of attendees, and the main goal(s) of the meeting in the notes.
- ☐ Assign tasks to meeting's members and write their names down next to the tasks; remember to announce tasks aloud to hold members accountable.
- ☐ After the meeting, immediately review the notes and update them for clarity, errors, and anything that was left out.
- ☐ Distribute notes promptly after the meeting, while the meeting is still fresh. This reminds people of their follow-up tasks.
- ☐ Have an agreed-upon place where meeting notes are stored (e.g., Dropbox, Slack).

Tool
MEETING EXPECTATIONS
QUICK SURVEY

I want our meetings to be an excellent use of your time. To that end, I have put together this one-minute survey. My hope is that spending one minute now will save us all lots of time later on. After I receive all the responses, I will look for underlying themes and share what I have learned with all of you.

1. As the facilitator of our meetings, what are key things you are looking for from me? What are your expectations?
2. What are the key things you are looking for from other attendees? What expectations do you have of others in our meetings?
3. Is there any other advice or are there key issues you want to convey, to help us have the best possible meetings we can?

ACKNOWLEDGMENTS

I am filled with gratitude to have so many wonderful people in my life supporting me and my work. Although my name is on the cover of the book, this was definitely not a solitary effort. First, I want to thank my agent, Jill Marsal, of Marsal Lyon Literary Agency, for her advocacy, professionalism, and tutelage. Next, I want to thank Abby Gross, Senior Editor at Oxford, for never wavering in her strong support of the book's concept and for her terrific responsiveness, very keen insights, and kindness every step of the way. Abby definitively made this book better! I am so fortunate to have had terrific doctoral students as partners from day one. Thank you to Miles Moffit and Claire Abberger for your sharp eye and strong input. I want to give a heartfelt special thanks to Lea Williams and Kelcie Grenier. I love it when I can learn from my students—your feedback, editing, and comments from the first page to last page elevated this entire effort. I also want to thank one of my mentors, Dr. John Kello, for not only reviewing sections of the book, but also being a model scientist-practitioner whose wisdom shaped many of my thoughts. Big thanks go to my life partner, Sandy Rogelberg, for supporting this entire effort from day one and for providing instrumental guidance throughout as she read the chapters and shared critical comments that greatly improved the content on these pages. I would be remiss if I did not thank my wonderful parents for just about everything, and for sharing their meeting war stories with me as I worked to prepare this book. And, thank you Sasha and Gordon for putting up with all of our family meetings. I love you both so much.

REFERENCES

Chapter 1
Caruth, R. L., & Caruth, G. D. (2012). Three prongs to manage meetings. *Industrial Management, 12–15.* Retrieved from https://www.questia.com/magazine/1P3-2849387751/three-prongs-to-manage-meetings

Doyle, M., & Straus, D. (1976). *How to make meetings work.* New York: Jove Books.

Executive Time Use Project. (2018). Retrieved from http://sticerd.lse.ac.uk/ExecutiveTimeUse/

Infocom. (n.d.). *Meetings in America: A study of trends, costs, and attitudes toward business travel and teleconferencing, and their impact on productivity.* Retrieved from https://e-meetings.verizonbusiness.com/global/en/meetingsinamerica/uswhitepaper.php

Keith, E. (2015, December 4). *55 million: A fresh look at the number, effectiveness, and cost of meetings in the U.S.* [Web log post]. Retrieved from http://blog.lucidmeetings.com/blog/fresh-look-number-effectiveness-cost-meetings-in-us

Malouff, J. M., Calic, C., McGrory, C. M., Murrell, R. L., & Schutte, N. S. (2012). Evidence for a needs-based model of organizational-meeting leadership. *Current Psychology, 31*(1), 35–48.

Microsoft. (2005, March 15). *Survey finds workers average only three productive days per week.* Retrieved from https://news.microsoft.com/2005/03/15/survey-finds-workers-average-only-three-productive-days-per-week/#sm.000006b85d5gudfpus7ro3hcg3jiy

Perlow, L. A., Hadley, C. N., & Eun, E. (2017). Stop the meeting madness. *Harvard Business Review, 95*(4), 62–69.

Rogelberg, S. G., Shanock, L. R., & Scott, C. W. (2012). Wasted time and money in meetings: Increasing return on investment. *Small Group Research, 43*(2), 236–45. doi:10.1177/1046496411429170

Romano, N. C., & Nunamaker, J. F. (2001, January). Meeting analysis: Findings from research and practice. In *System Sciences, 2001. Proceedings of the 34th Annual Hawaii International Conference on System Sciences*, Maui, Hawaii. doi:10.1109/HICSS.2001.

Chapter 2

Allen, J. A., & Rogelberg, S. G. (2013). Manager-led group meetings: A context for promoting employee engagement. *Group & Organization Management, 38*(5), 543–569.

Barsade, S. G. (2002). The ripple effect: Emotional contagion and its influence on group behavior. *Administrative Science Quarterly, 47*(4), 644–675.

Bluedorn, A. C., Turban, D. C., & Love, M. S. (1999). The effects of stand-up and sit-down meeting formats on meeting outcomes. *Journal of Applied Psychology, 84*(2), 277–285.

Goldman, J. (2016, March 21). 13 insightful quotes from Intel visionary Andy Grove. *Inc.* http://www.inc.com/jeremy-goldman/13-insightful-quotes-from-intel-visionary-andy-grove.html

Rogelberg, S. G., Leach, D. J., Warr, P. B., & Burnfield, J. L. (2006). "Not another meeting!" Are meeting time demands related to employee well-being? *Journal of Applied Psychology, 91*(1), 83–96.

Chapter 3

Cohen, J. (2016, September 12). Use subtle cues to encourage better meetings. *Harvard Business Review.* Retrieved from https://hbr.org/2016/09/use-subtle-cues-to-encourage-better-meetings

College Board. (1976–1977). *Student descriptive questionnaire.* Princeton, NJ: Educational Testing Service.

Cross, K. P. (1977). Not can, but will college teaching be improved? *New Directions for Higher Education, 1977*(17), 1–15.

Flaum, J. P. (2009). When it comes to business leadership, nice guys finish first. *Talent Management Online.*

Grant, A. (2013, April). In the company of givers and takers. *Harvard Business Review.* Retrieved from https://hbr.org/2013/04/in-the-company-of-givers-and-takers

Infocom. (n.d.). *Meetings in America: A study of trends, costs, and attitudes toward business travel and teleconferencing, and their impact on productivity.* Retrieved from https://e-meetings.verizonbusiness.com/global/en/meetingsinamerica/uswhitepaper.php

Malouff, J. M., Calic, A., McGrory, C. M., Murrell, R. L., & Schutte, N. S. (2012). Evidence for a needs-based model of organizational-meeting leadership. *Current Psychology, 31*(1), 35–48.

Myers, D. G. (1995). Humility: Theology meets psychology. *Reformed Review, 48*(3), 195–206.

Sedikides, C., Gaertner, L., & Vevea, J. L. (2005). Pancultural self-enhancement reloaded: A meta-analytic reply to Heine (2005). *Journal of Personality and Social Psychology, 89*(4), 539–551.

Sedikides, C., Meek, R., Alicke, M. D., & Taylor, S. (2014). Behind bars but above the bar: Prisoners consider themselves more prosocial than non-prisoners. *British Journal of Social Psychology, 53*(2), 396–403.

Chapter 4

Bryan, J. F., & Locke, E. A. (1967). Parkinson's law as a goal-setting phenomenon. *Organizational Behavior and Human Performance, 2*(3), 258–275.

Buchanan, L. (2007, November 1). The art of the huddle. *Inc.* Retrieved from http://www.inc.com/magazine/20071101/the-art-of-the-huddle.html

D'Alessio, S. J., & Stolzenberg, L. (1997). The effect of available capacity on jail incarceration: An empirical test of Parkinson's law. *Journal of Criminal Justice, 25*(4), 279–288.

Parkinson, C. N., & Osborn, R. C. (1957). *Parkinson's law, and other studies in administration* (Vol. 24). Boston: Houghton Mifflin. Also see http://www.economist.com/node/14116121

Satish, U., Mendell, M. J., Shekhar, K., Hotchi, T., Sullivan, D., Streufert, S., & Fisk, W. J. (2012). Is CO_2 an indoor pollutant? Direct effects of low-to-moderate CO_2 concentrations on human decision-making performance. *Environmental Health Perspectives, 120*(12), 1671–1677.

Chapter 5

Littlepage, G. E., & Poole, J. R. (1993). Time allocation in decision making groups. *Journal of Social Behavior and Personality, 8*(4), 663–672.

Mankins, M. C. (2004). Stop wasting valuable time. *Harvard Business Review, 82*(9), 58–67.

Chapter 6

Aubé, C., Rousseau, V., & Tremblay, S. (2011). Team size and quality of group experience: The more the merrier? *Group Dynamics: Theory, Research, and Practice, 15*(4), 357–375.

Gallo, C. (2006, September 27). How to run a meeting like Google. *Bloomberg,* https://www.bloomberg.com/news/articles/2006-09-26/how-to-run-a-meeting-like-google

Guéguen, N., Dupré, M., Georget, P., & Sénémeaud, C. (2015). Commitment, crime, and the responsive bystander: Effect of the commitment form and conformism. *Psychology, Crime & Law, 21*(1), 1–8.

Harvard Business Review. (2014). *Running meetings (20-minute manager series)* [R-reader version]. Retrieved from https://hbr.org/product/running-meetings-20-minute-manager-series/17003E-KND-ENG

Ingham, A. G., Levinger, G., Graves, J., & Peckham, V. (1974). The Ringelmann effect: Studies of group size and group performance. *Journal of Experimental Social Psychology, 10*(4), 371–384.

Chapter 7

Bluedorn, A. C., Turban, D. B., & Love, M. S. (1999). The effects of stand-up and sit-down meeting formats on meeting outcomes. *Journal of Applied Psychology, 84*(2), 277–285.

Clayton, R., Thomas, C., & Smothers, J. (2015, August 5). How to do walking meetings right. *Harvard Business Review*. Retrieved from https://hbr.org/2015/08/how-to-do-walking-meetings-right

Economy, P. (2017, May 1). 7 powerful reasons to take your next meeting for a walk. *Inc.* Retrieved from https://www.inc.com/peter-economy/7-powerful-reasons-to-take-your-next-meeting-for-a-walk.html

Knight, A. P., & Baer, M. (2014). Get up, stand up: The effects of a non-sedentary workspace on information elaboration and group performance. *Social Psychological and Personality Science, 5*(8), 910–917.

Neal, D. T., Wood, W., & Quinn, J. M. (2006). Habits—A repeat performance. *Current Directions in Psychological Science, 15*(4), 198–202.

Oppezzo, M., & Schwartz, D. L. (2014). Give your ideas some legs: The positive effect of walking on creative thinking. *Journal of Experimental Psychology: Learning, Memory, and Cognition, 40*(4), 1142–1152.

Veerman, J. L., Healy, G. N., Cobiac, L. J., Vos, T., Winkler, E. A., Owen, N., & Dunstan, D. W. (2011). Television viewing time and reduced life expectancy: A life table analysis. *British Journal of Sports Medicine, 46*(13), 927–930.

Chapter 8

Grawitch, M. J., Munz, D. C., Elliott, E. K., & Mathis, A. (2003). Promoting creativity in temporary problem-solving groups: The effects of positive mood and autonomy in problem definition on idea-generating performance. *Group Dynamics: Theory, Research, and Practice, 7*(3), 200–213.

Karlesky, M., & Isbister, K. (2014, February). Designing for the physical margins of digital workspaces: Fidget widgets in support of productivity and creativity. In *Proceedings of the 8th International Conference on Tangible, Embedded and Embodied Interaction, Munich, Germany* (pp. 13–20). doi:10.1145/2540930.2540978

Lehmann-Willenbrock, N., & Allen, J. A. (2014). How fun are your meetings? Investigating the relationship between humor patterns in team interactions and team performance. *Journal of Applied Psychology, 99*(6), 1278–1287.

Mueller, P. A., & Oppenheimer, D. M. (2014). The pen is mightier than the keyboard: Advantages of longhand over laptop note taking. *Psychological Science, 25*(6), 1159–1168.

Rogelberg, S. G., Barnes-Farrell, J. L., & Lowe, C. A. (1992). The stepladder technique: An alternative group structure facilitating effective group decision making. *Journal of Applied Psychology, 77*(5), 730–737.

Technology addiction 101. (2015). *Addiction.com*. Retrieved from https://www.addiction.com/addiction-a-to-z/technology-addiction/technology-addiction-101/

Washington, M. C., Okoro, E. A., & Cardon, P. W. (2014). Perceptions of civility for mobile phone use in formal and informal meetings. *Business and Professional Communication Quarterly, 77*(1), 52–64.

Zijlstra, F. R., Waller, M. J., & Phillips, S. I. (2012). Setting the tone: Early interaction patterns in swift-starting teams as a predictor of effectiveness. *European Journal of Work and Organizational Psychology, 21*(5), 749–777.

Chapter 9

Gallupe, R. B., Dennis, A. R., Cooper, W. H., Valacich, J. S., Bastianutti, L. M., & Nunamaker, J. F. (1992). Electronic brainstorming and group size. *Academy of Management Journal, 35*(2), 350–369.

Heslin, P. A. (2009). Better than brainstorming? Potential contextual boundary conditions to brainwriting for idea generation in organizations. *Journal of Occupational and Organizational Psychology, 82*(1), 129–45.

Rogelberg, S. G., Barnes-Farrell, J. L., & Lowe, C. A. (1992). The stepladder technique: An alternative group structure facilitating effective group decision making. *Journal of Applied Psychology, 77*(5), 730–737.

Stasser, G., & Titus, W. (1985). Pooling of unshared information in group decision making: Biased information sampling during discussion. *Journal of Personality and Social Psychology, 48*(6), 1467–1478.

Williams, K., Harkins, S. G., & Latané, B. (1981). Identifiability as a deterrent to social loafing: Two cheering experiments. *Journal of Personality and Social Psychology, 40*(2), 303–311.

Chapter 10

Maier, N. R. F., & Hoffman, L. R. (1960). Quality of first and second solutions in group problem solving. *Journal of Applied Psychology, 44,* 278–283.

Mankins, M. (2004, September). Stop wasting valuable time. *Harvard Business Review.* Retrieved from https://hbr.org/2004/09/stop-wasting-valuable-time

Rogelberg, S. G., O'Connor, M. S., & Sederburg, M. (2002). Using the stepladder technique to facilitate the performance of audioconferencing. *Journal of Applied Psychology, 87*(5), 994–1000.

INDEX

Page numbers followed by *f* and *t* refer to figures and tables, respectively.